Land Entries

of

Jackson County Tennessee
- 1802-1805 -
and
Davidson County Tennessee
- 1802-1803 -

Compiled by:
Dr. Albert Bruce Pruitt

Southern Historical Press
Greenville, South Carolina

This volume was reproduced
from a personal copy located in
the Publishers private library

Please direct all correspondence and book orders to:
www.southernhistoricalpress.com
or
SOUTHERN HISTORICAL PRESS, Inc.
1071 Park West Blvd.
Greenville, SC   29611

Southernhistoricalpress@gmail.com

Introduction

This book contains entries or locations in an office in Jackson County [Record Group 50, series 2 book 54, roll 17 (1802-1805) items 1-239] and office in Davidson County [Record Group 50, series 2, book 55, roll 17 (1802-1803), items 240-377].

In 1802, the North Carolina Assembly passed an act saying no more grants in Tennessee. Because of that ac t, the Tennessee Assembly believed it was time to begin recording entries in county offices in Tennessee, and they expected Congress to pass an act allowing Tennessee to issue grants. But Congress failed to pas the necessary act. So some Tennessee county offices stopped recording entries in 1803 (like Davidson County), but some continued to record entries to 1805 (like Jackson County). Paperwork from similarly offices have been found for Washington County (in Archives of Appalachia at East Tennessee State Univ. in Johnson City, Tennessee, published with other Washington County entries in 207) and Smith County (in Tennessee Archives, published with first volume of First Surveyor's District in 2008). There may be additional books still I county court houses. Since Tennessee wasn't allowed to issue grants in 1803 and 1804, some people petitioned the North Carolina Assembly individually asking for a grant; and North Carolina did issue a few grants I 1803 and 184 (shucks 2471 & 2472 in Davidson County and shuck 1468 in Sumner County and shuck 1384 in Washington County (in NC grants in Tennessee). In 1806, Congress finally passes an act allowing Tennessee to issue grants. While most of the entries prior to 1805 were never used, some (mentioned I this book) in Davidson County were sold, and the new owner used them to make entries in the First Surveyor's District and obtain grants from Tennessee. There was a brief attempt by North Carolina to issue grants in the Second Surveyor's District in 1812-1815, but these grants were voided by decision of US Supreme Court in 1818.

Thanks to Lindsay Hagler and Ronald A Lee, of the Tennessee Archives, for help making copies of pages missing from the microfilm.

Land Entries of Jackson County & Davidson County, TN (1802-1803)

Jackson County [series 2 book 54, roll 17]
      index for letters B through Z at front of book

p. 1
1. Mar. 9, 1802 John Raybourn; "no warrant for this location"; 640 ac of his settlement on Flat Cr, a branch of "R" River, begins at beech on E side of the creek, runs N30W 60 poles to 3 black oaks marked "J R", S60W 80 poles, N60E 80 poles to the creek, up the creek and E from beginning for complement.

2. Mar. 9, 1802 James Lock; "no warrant for this location"; 200 ac in Jackson Co on Jennings Cr, about 1.25 miles below the big spring, begins at beech & elm on the creek bank, runs West down the creek with first line, & runs as law directs.

p. 2
3. Mar. 9, 1802 Garret Fitzgerald; warrant 1932; 170 ac on Doe Cr, runs up & down for complement, "encludes" Armstrong's & Gourd's improvement; made void by order of "Gorret" Fitzgerald Aug. 1, 1802.

4. Mar. 9, 1802 Garret Fitzgerald; warrant 1932; 370 [written over 640] ac on dividing ridge between Doe Cr & Flyns Cr, includes my improvement on the ridge "an" a pond.

p. 3
5. Mar. 9, 1802 Garret Fitzgerald; warrant 1457; 270 (100 ac also mentioned) ac in Jackson Co, on E side of Flynns Cr, joins his own lines, runs law law directs.

6. Mar. 9, 1802 John Russell; "no warrant for this location"; 300 ac, joins William Russell in Jackson Co, runs as law directs.

7. Mar. 9, 1802 Henry Reybourn; "no warrant for this location"; 200 ac on Flat Cr, eastern waters of "R" River, begins at "formedable" corner of John Reybourn's near a bluff of laurel on E side of Flat Cr, runs up said creek and up West fork of said creek, near Thompson's fence, E, S for complement.

p. 4
8. Mar. 9, 1802 Richd Batton; "no warrant for this location";
200 ac on a South branch of Spring Cr, in Jackson Co, begins on E side of the creek at a black oak, runs up said creek, & includes said Batton's improvement.

9. Mar. 9, 1802 Joseph Russell; "no warrant for this location"; 640 ac on waters of Jennings Cr, in Jackson Co; joins Buckner Russell line on "the" West boundary line, runs as law directs for complement, includes said Russell's improvement.

10. Mar. 10, 1802 Joseph Lock; "no warrant for this location"; 640 ac in Jackson Co, begins at an elm & 2 sycamores being Thaner's corner on N side of

Cumberland R about 200 yards above mouth of Roaring R, runs along said Thaner's line, includes part of large knob, then up the river for complement, & as the law directs.

p. 5
11. Mar. 10, 1802 Joseph Lock; "no warrant for this location"; 200 ac in Jackson Co, on S side of Cumberland R, begins a Hickman's S line, runs up the creek for complement as law directs.

12. Mar. 12, 1802 Garret Fitzgerald; 200 ac in Jackson Co, on Doe Cr, begins above Armstrong's improvement, runs down both sides of said creek.13. Mar. 12, 1802 Garret Fitzgerald, assignee of William Mutherreizes [or Meetherreizes] John Page; warrant 1432; 50 ac in Jackson Co on a branch of Doe Cr, begins at the fork [written over "foot"] of Hurricane Ridge, runs down said branch, includes James Isham's spring & improvement; [the remainder not specified––lined out].

14. Mar. 12, 1802 David Harbert; "no warrant for this location"; 400 ac in Jackson Co on dividing ridge between Flinn's Cr and Roaring R, joins Garret Fitzgerald's entry on South, runs as law directs for complement; David Harbert locator.

15. Mar. 12, 1802 John Houser; "no warrant for this location"; 640 ac in Jackson Co, on dividing ridge between Flinn's Cr and Roaring R, where said Houser lives, runs as law directs for complement; John Houser locator.

p. 6
16. Mar. 16, 1802 Thomas Taylor; "no warrant for this location"; 640 ac on waters of "R" River, begins at 2 post oaks out of one root marked "T T" standing on Jas Taylor's SW line in the barrens, runs S150E (sic) with said line, S55W, bounding with Wm Pryor lines for complement; located Mar. 13, 1802 by John Sullivan.

17. Mar. 16, 1802 Benjamin Ford; "no warrant for this location"; 150 ac on waters of Cumberland R, begins on Cave Spring Br, joins Henry McKenny's line, runs up both sides of the creek for complement.

18. Mar. 19, 1802 David & John Womack; "no warrant for this location"; 640 ac in Jackson Co, on E fork of Russel mill Cr, begins at a cedar on a bluff on said creek below "compt shr" running westwardly to join Prior's line, includes Sink hole Spring and improvement where said Womack lives, runs to include content between James Taylor & Womack, & runs as law directs for complement.

19. Mar. 19, 1802 Garret Fitzgerald; "no warrant for this location"; 50 ac in Jackson Co, on S side of Cumberland R, begins on my own line on the river, runs up the river for complement as law directs.

20. Mar. 20, 1802 Joseph Pryor, assignee of William Dalton; [no warrant for this

location--lined out] military warrant (blank); 460 ac on E fork of S fork of Roaring R, begins at 2 post oaks on N side of said creek, runs S, & E for complement.

21. Mar. 20, 1802 John Fitzgerald; "no warrant for this location"; 200 ac in Jackson Co, on Doe Cr, joins Garret Fitzgerald's entry that goes by name "Gord's" improvement, joins said improvement on N, runs down each sie of said creek as law directs for complement.

22. Mar. 22, 1802 William Robertson; "no warrant for this location"; 100 ac on a small branch of Roaring R where there is a small "pen" made and some sugar trees tapped, begins on the branch 35 poles above said pen, runs down the branch for complement, includes said pen and sugar trees that "is" tapped; "locatee".

23. Mar. 22, 1802 William Robertson; "no warrant for this location"; 100 ac on the creek that he lives on, begins on said creek 40 poles above a large spring, runs down the creek for complement, includes said spring & a small improvement; William Rosset(maybe) locator.

24. Mar. 25, 1802 John McNairy, purchases at sheriff's sale of James Cole Mountflorence assignee of George Walker of Richard Fenner of said Mountflorence of John McNees of heirs of William Hamm; warrant 2100 [warrant in Tennessee Revolutionary War warrants roll 4]; 640 ac in Jackson Co, S of Gelston's tract, begins at white & red oak marked "F &c" being beginning corner of Moses Fisk's location entered May 1801 on warrant 4132, about 110 poles W of NW corner of 640 ac tract that includes improvement McLane got of Goodpasture and now lives on, extends North by said Fisk's line to Gelston's line, W to include said 640 ac "fit for cultivation" exclusive of prior claims; Moses Fisk locator.

25. Mar. 25, 1802 William Tyrrell Lewis, assignee of Stockley Donelson of Isaiah Carr; warrant 5193; 640 ac in Jackson Co on head waters of Sugar Cr; begins at chesnut & poplar marked by Capt. Williams in Apr. 1800 as "mile" trees being a mile West of his 13 mile tree, then marked by h im surveying for John Love, above location to run from said beginning West & South to best advantage the law will allow, includes said 640 ac fit for cultivation, exclusive of prior claims; Moses Fisk locator.

p. 9

26. Mar. 25, 1802 Edward Harris, assignee of Henry Bonner executor & devisee of James & John Bonner assignees of heirs of Solomon Overton; warrant 3017 [warrant in Tennessee Revolutionary War warrants roll 4]; 1,000 ac in Jackson on head waters of Sugar Cr & waters of Roaring R; begins 80 poles SE of blazed red oak that stands on a ridge beside the path from Hutcheson's towards Mr. Ewing's "&c", said blazed oak being line tree in S boundary of 640 ac on which John

Hutcheson jr has settled as "run for trial" by Moses Fisk, Benjamin Stowell &c sometime in Dec. last, above location then to extend from said beginning West & South to best advantage the law will allow, includes 1,000 ac of land fit for cultivation exclusive of prior claims; Moses Fisk locator.

27. Mar. 25, 1802 William T Lewis, assignee of Stockley Donelson of heirs of Alexander Cotter; warrant 5174; 640 ac in Jackson Co on head waters of Sampson's Fork and some of branches of Roaring R; begins at sugar tree "a few" poles northeasterly of camp on the ridge near where path from David Mitchell's to Hutcheson's and another from Black's to Hutcheson's meet, extends N, S, & S to include 640 ac of land fit of cultivation, exclusive of prior claims; Moses Fisk locator; made void by order of Moses Fisk.

p. 10
28. Apr. 9, 1802 William Hale; warrant (blank); 170 ac in Jackson Co on Doe Cr, begins above Armstrong's & Gord's improvement, runs down said creek to include said improvement to best advantage agreeable to law; [comments in margin erased].

29. Apr. 16, 1802 Ephraim Payton, assignee of "Thomos" Kenney; certificate by John Payton that grant No. 156 was lost [no warrant mentioned]; 480 ac on S side of Cumberland R, begins on or at mouth of creek known as Sugar Run, on both sides of said creek, & up and down the river for complement as law directs; this warrant removed & entered on p. 47 [item number 110], this entry made void by order from "Ephram" Payton.

30. May 22, 1802 Ambose Gore, assignee of Thomas Elliott of Joel Dyer; warrant 2288; 500 ac on head waters of Copelands Cr, a branch of Roaring R, begins at a poplar on N side of a hill, runs as law directs to include his improvement and said complement; made void by order of "Ambrus" Gore Mar. 21, 1804.

31. May 22, 1802 William Allen, assignee of James Moore of Jacob "Woork"; warrant 418; 200 ac on W side of Flat Cr, begins at black oak marked "W A" on top of the ridge between said "creeks", runs as law directs, includes his improvement & complement; James Taylor locator.

p. 11
32. May 22, 1802 James Taylor for Nathaniel Taylor; warrant 82; 250 ac in Jackson Co on head waters of E fork of Flat Cr, a branch of Roaring R, begins at chesnut & oak marked "N T" near a path, runs as law directs to include a cove known as Sugar Cove and said complement fit for cultivation, exclusive of prior claims; James Taylor locator; "coppy esued".

33. May 22, 1802 Jacob Work; warrant 211; 150 ac in Jackson Co on creek known as Lamb's Cr, a branch of Roaring R, begins at 2 black oaks standing on W side

of path from said creek to Flat Cr, runs as law directs, includes an improvement where Joseph Copeland lives & said complement; Jas Taylor locator; copy erased.

34. May 22, 1802 Jacob Work; warrant 275; 300 ac in Jackson Co on E fok of Flat Cr waters of Roaring R, begins at a white oak near head of a spring known as Rocky Spring, on W side of said creek, runs as law directs to include Robert Seypart's improvement and said complement, exclusive of pryor claims and land fit for cultivation; Jas Taylor locator; coppy esued.

p. 12
35. May 22, 1802 Nathaniel Taylor; warrant 108; 350 ac in Jackson Co on waters of Roaring R, begins at oak & poplar marked "N T" standing near a branch known as Waltons Br, runs as law directs to include a salt petre cave & said complement; coppy esued.

36. May 22, 1802 James Taylor, for Thos Michison; warrant 220; 213 1/3 ac "if" said Thos "Mickson" & said James Taylor agrees and "Mickinson" buys said warrant and if not the entry stands in name of Nathaniel Taylor; on waters of Roaring R, joins Watson's tract, begins at 2 post oaks on line of his, runs as law directs for complement, includes said complement fit for cultivation, exclusive of prior claims; Jas Taylor locator; this entry "set voyd" by order of James Taylor.

37. May 22, 1802 James Taylor, for Thomas Mickinson; warrant 220 from Adair's office; 213 1/3 ac, if said Thos Mickinson and said James Taylor agrees and "Mickison" buys said warrant and if not the entry stands in name of Nathaniel Taylor; on waters of Roaring R, joins Watson's tract, begins at red oak & post oak, runs as law directs for complement; James Taylor locator; this entry "set voyd" by order of James Taylor.

p. 13
38. May 22, 1802 James Taylor for Thomas Mickinson; warrant 220 from Adair's office; 213 1/3 ac, if said Thos Mickinson & said James Taylor agrees and said Mickinson buys said warrant and if not the entry stands in name of Nathaniel Taylor; on waters of Roaring R, joins Watson's tract, begins at 2 post oaks, runs as law directs for complement, exclusive of prior claims, and land that is fit for cultivation; Jas Taylor locator; this entry "set void" by order of Jas Taylor.

39. May 22, 1802 James Taylor, for Nathaniel Taylor; warrant 119; 640 ac in Jackson Co on waters of Roaring R; begins at large post oak marked "W F" standing up the valley above where Wm Fitzgarald lives on side of the ridge, runs as law directs to include improvements where William Fitzgerald lives and others with said complement fit for cultivation, exclusive of prior claims; James Taylor locator; coppy issued.

p. 14

40. Jun. 28, 1802 Isaac Taylor, for Nathaniel Taylor & co; warrant 84 from Adair's office; 400 ac on waters of Roaring R, begins at black oak & white oak, the white oak marked "N T" standing on N side of small branch, runs SW with "the" Indian line for complement, not interfering wit Indian land; coppy "esued".

41. Jul. 2, 1802 David & John Womack, assignees of William Robertson; part of Armstrong's warrant 1642; 350 ac in Jackson Co on waters of Roaring R, begins on W side, runs W to Wevor's claim, S to "Jonston" Womack bounds, E to include improvements were said "Womak" lives; "Mar. 25" I transfer 300 ac of this entry by order of David & John Womack to "Leram Jackson Charles Moguire" (signed) John "Fitzgerd".

42. Jul. 5, 1802 Christopher "Bullar", assignee of Sampson Williams, heirs of John McNees of Benjamin Powell; warrant 508; 640 ac on N side of Cumberland R, begins at mouth of a small creek above where he lives called Trace Cr, runs up and down the river for complement; "Chrstophr" locator; I transfer 320 ac being upper end;

       [on loose sheet] Aug. 7, 1805 I transfer 320 ac to Edmund Roberts, being half of 640 ac entry in John Fitzgerald's book page 14 location 42, it is upper half of said entry, without any "recorse" back to me (signed) "Chrstopher" Ballard (witness) William Roberson [and see last 2 items in book].

p. 15
43. Jul. 9, 1802 Moses Fisk, assignee of Sampson Williams of Stockley Donelson & Will Tyrrell of heirs of John Keith; [military] warrant 3635; 640 ac in Jackson Co on waters of Roaring R, between E fork & the ridge that divided its waters from those of Sampson's Fork of Mill Cr, includes "best part" of a flat that lies westerly of path from old Mr. "Officer's" to Capt. Mitchell's, begins about 90 poles NW of an oak marked "J O" that stands close by a pen "made perhaps" to catch turkies, from said beginning extends E & S to cover said 640 ac of land fit for cultivation, exclusive of prior claims, John Bowen esquire was present with said Fisk as said pen & oak marked "J O" on 6th instant "namely" Jul. 6, 1802; Moses Fisk locator.

44. Jul. 9, 1802 John & Robert Allen, assignees of Benjamin McFarland; [military] warrant 4328; 274 ac in Jackson Co on a westerly branch of Dry Cr, which Dry Cr empties into E fork of Roaring R, location to include a spring by which are 2 beeches marked "F" and "several" trees blazed and some deadened, includes the rich cane land, said spring to be a few poles North westerly of center of the tract; Moses Fisk locator.

p. 16
45. Jul. 26, 1802 Moses Fisk, assignee of Stockeley Donelson of heirs of James R Whitney; [military] warrant 3960; 640 ac in Jackson Co on the highlands South of Sampson's Fork of Mill Cr, begins 120 poles S of 13 mile tree marked by Capt.

Williams in Apr. 1800 to denote distance from intersection of state line with Cumberland R in "magnetic" South course, runs E & S to include plantation on which George Hutcheson, "his mother &c" live, includes 640 ac fit for cultivation, exclusive of prior claims; Moses Fisk locator; [altered & "solim" page 76 location 169-lined out]; revize & "sotin" p. 85 [location 187].

46. Jul. 26, 1802 David Henley, assignee of John Overton of Redmond D Barry of heirs of John Seagraves; [military] warrant 4215; 40 ac on W fork of Roaring R, joins tract John Richmond lives on "above", runs up both sides of said fork for complement; S Williams locator.

p. 17
47. Aug. 3, 1802 David Ramsey, assignee of James T Gaines; warrant 16; 100 ac begins on E side of of said Ramsey's other entry, runs "divers corses" to include my spring & "emproveemnt" with 100 ac where I "know" live; David Ramsey locator.

48. Aug. 3, 1802 David Ramsey, assignee of James T Gaines; warrant 16 from "Adear" office; 140 ac, begins on William Russel's line on S fork of his mill creek, runs up "sade" creek "neer" South "corse" to include John Russel's improvement where he "know" lives; David Ramsey locator.

49. Aug. 5, 1802 Jesse "Oldrhey", assignee of Thomas Megginson of Barton Scrogins of "Rusell" Been; warrant 467; 100 ac in Jackson Co on middle fork of Roaring R, joins Russell's on E side, begins at black walnut on Rusell's line in said Starkey's corn field, runs as law directs for complement; Jessey Starkey locator.

p. 18
50. Aug. 5, 1802 Nathaniel Taylor, assignee of Malowre (or Malore) Mecown; warrant 13; 640 ac in Jackson Co on S side of N fork of Roaring R, begins at 3 post oaks on E side of a path, runs N & E for complement; Thomas Taylor locator; coppy "esued".

51. Aug. 5, 1802 Jacob Work, assignee of John Scott; "Adear" warrant 508 to John Scott; 250 ac in Jackson Co, on waters of "Roreing" R, begins at black "oack" marked "Ɨ" [and] several post oaks standing on S side of a path from William Bryor's to John Bryor's, runs W & N for complement; coppy issued.

52. Aug. 5, 1804 Nathaniel Taylor, assignee of John Winegam [or Wargam, or Worgarn]; warrant 201; 640 ac on head of "cartarn" branch of "Roarng" R, joins Ambrous Gore's entry, runs as law directs, includes said complement fit for cultivation, exclusive of "pryer" claims; James Taylor locator; coppy issued.

p. 19

53. Aug. 5, 1802 Nathaniel Taylor; warrant 219 from Adair's office; 640 ac in Jackson Co on head of and eastern branch of "Roreing" R, begins at a beach, oak & "shuger" tree in small valley near the foot of a rocky mountain, runs S, & W for complement; James Taylor locator; coppy issued.

54. Aug. 5, 1802 Jacob Work, assignee of "Moloan Mccown" [Malcom McCown in entry book]; warrant 421 from Adair's office; 640 ac on waters of "Roreing" R, in Jackson Co, begins at a black oak & post oak o the "Indion" line between 54 and 55 mile trees on a ridge, runs W, as law directs for complement, includes said complement fit for cultivation, exclusive of "prier" claims; James Taylor locator.

p. 20
55. Aug. 5, 1802 Nathaniel Taylor, assignee of David "Gront" of "Maylon" Thompson; military warrant 3761; 640 ac in "Jacktion" Co, on S fork of "Rorein" R, begins at spanish oak & 2 hickory saplins standing in a flat, runs E & S for complement, includes the improvement of [blank]; James Taylor locator; copy issued.

56. Aug. 5, 1802 Joseph Coplan, assignee of Stephen Copland [or Coapland]; warrant 691 from Adair's office; 400 ac in Jackson Co on Copelands Cr, on eastern branch of Roaring R, begins at double sycamore on S branch of said creek, runs S & W with conditional lines for complement; Stephen Coapland locator.

57. Aug. 5, 1802 William Tilghman; military warrant 1101; 274 ac in "Jacktion" Co on S side of Roaring R, begins at 2 white oaks & a black oak, runs E & S, includes "Alaxander" Ivrin's [or Tvrin] improvement 'by consent" for complement; William Tilghman locator.

p. 21
58. Aug. 5, 1802 John Gray Blount, assignee of "haeirs" of Benjamin Sanders; military warrant 104; 40 ac in Jackson Co on waters of Roaring R, begins at 2 hickorys & gum marked "J T" near the Indian boundary, runs E & N for complement; Thomas Dillen locator.

59. Aug. 5, 1802 John G [Blount] & James Porterfield, heir of Demy Porterfield; warrant 100; 3,840 (sic) ac in Jackson Co on middle fork of Roaring R; begins at black oak & white oak on N side of said fork on a ridge, runs N & E for complement; Thomas Dillen locator.

p. 22
60. Aug. 5, 1802 Wm Shepherd; military warrant 3553; 1,252 ac in Jackson Co on W fork of Sugar Cr, begins at 2 sugar trees on S side of the creek, runs N & E for complement; Thomas Dillen locator.

61. Aug. 5, 1802 Edwd Harris, assignee of Malachy Russell; warrant 637; 640 ac in Jackson Co on Doe Cr, a branch of Roaring R, begins at 2 beeches near mouth of said creek on E side, runs S & E for complement; Thomas Dillen locator.

p. 23
62. Aug. 5, 1802 Jno Morriss, heir of "Ben"; warrant 1476; 640 ac in Jackson Co on middle fork of Roaring R, begins at white oak, sugar tree & hickory, runs W & N for complement; Thomas Dillen locator.

63. Aug. 5, 1802 heirs of Wm Haynes; warrant 39; 640 ac in Jackson Co on waters of Roaring R, begins at 3 hickory saplins on Russell's line [written over "land"], runs S & E for complement; Thomas Dillen locator.

p. 24
64. Aug. 5, 1802 heirs of Solomon "Mobborn"; military warrant 4447; 1,000 ac in Jackson Co on head of an eastern branch of Roaring R, begins at white oak on a hill side, runs N 370 poles to large poplar, & E for complement; Thomas Dillen locator.

65. Aug. 5, 1802 Mordica Mendenhall, of Lot Stroud; warrant 38; 228 ac in Jackson Co on waters of Roaring R; begins at large poplar on N side of a hill, runs N & E for complement; Thomas "Dillan" locator.

p. 25
66. Aug. 5, 1802 Wm Person, assignee of heirs of Luke Fenner [or Tumer]; military warrant 3383; 640 ac in Jackson Co on waters of middle fork of Roaring R, begins at 2 black oaks at head of a hollow corner of Wm Russell's land, runs N 227 poles crossing a branch to a poplar, E, & S for complement; Thomas Dillen locator; warrant is "lifted" and "assignee" to Garret Fitzgerald and from Fitzgerald to John "Tolly" he enters warrant on p. 46 [108]; made void by Thomas Dillen.

67. Aug. 6, 1802 Nathaniel Taylor assignee of Samuel Donals; warrant 210 for Adair's office; 60 ac in Jackson Co on waters of middle fork of "Rorring" R, begins at several post oaks standing W of a "bold running" branch, a small distance S of a path, runs as law directs, includes an improvement & said complement fit for cultivation, exclusive of "pryor" claims; James Taylor locator.

p. 26
68. Aug. 6, 1802 Joseph "Prior", assignee of William Robertson; part of warrant 1642 from John Armstrong's office for 1,000 ac; 150 ac in Jackson Co on W fork of Russels mill Cr, a branch of Roaring R, begins at a post oak near a path from said Pryar's to John Starky's, runs as law directs to include said Pryor's improvement & complement; Joseph Pryor locator.

69. Aug. 9, 1802 William Robertson, assignee of heirs of Charles Robertson

deceased; warrant 1642 from John Armstrong's office; 300 ac in Jackson Co on Spring Cr, a branch of Roaring R, begins at a post oak on the Indian line, runs S, down the creek, & includes Cline's improvement and said complement; William Robertson locator; "sot" void by William Robertson.

p. 27
70. Sept. 11, 1802 "no names to this location Hrs entry jund in name of Tyler"; warrant 375; 100 ac on waters of Roaring R, begins at black oak on N side of the river runs N to conditional line, with said line "round" as law directs for complement, includes Herty's improvement, now in my possession Benjamin Blackburn; made void by Benjamin Blackburn.

71. Sept. 11, 1802 Moses Fisk, assignee of James T Gaines; warrant 16; 200 ac in Jackson Co on W of land entered for Robert "Cortwright", joins same, & includes improvement of John Black; Moses Fisk locator.

p. 28
72. Sept. 11, 1802 Moses Fisk, assignee of James T Gaines; warrant 16; 200 ac in Jackson Co on waters of "Coperace" Cr sometimes called Dry Cr of Roaring R, begins 10 poles NW of a white oak, 3 beeches & 3 small poplars marked "ef E" standing at or near head of a hollow of NW fork that comes into Coperos Cr at cascades, runs E, & S for quantity; Moses Fisk locator.

73. Sept. 11, 1802 Moses Fisk, assignee of "Sokly" Donelson of James Chissum; [military] warrant 3954; 640 ac on waters of Roaring R, begins at 7 white oaks SW of path from old "Mr. Officer's" to Captain Mitchell's, runs W 160 poles, N 320 poles, & E for quantity; Moses Fisk locator.

p. 29
74. Sept. 11, 1802 Moses Fisk, assignee of James T Gaines; warrant 15; 640 ac S of Gilston track "so called" which is part of 60,400 ac grant to Stockley Donelson in 1795 [maybe shuck 508 in Eastern Dist, in NC grants], includes mouth of "Oby" R, joins southern boundary of said track & W boundary of 640 ac surveyed for Samuel Sanford, begins at white oak near head of a spring; Moses Fisk locator.

75. Sept. 17, 1802 Redmond Dillon Barry, assignee of James Timons son of Raymond Jones; [military] warrant 4223 for 640 ac; 300 ac on Styns Cr in Jackson Co, begins at large poplar near road running oblong up the creek, between said Barry's 2 entries on warrants 4060 & 1923 for 228 ac each entered in Martin Armstrong's office in 1797 [no grants by NC identified for these 2 warrants], this 300 ac is balance of warrant 4223; Redmond Dillon Barry locator.

p. 30
76. Sept 17, 1802 Uriah Anderson; [miliary] warrant 4046; 100 ac on waters of Roaring R, includes improvement where Joseph Weaver lives, which

improvement was first made by Jacob Harty, below Benjamin Blackbourn's; Uriah Anderson locator.

77. Sept. 17, 1802 James Taylor, assignee of Thomas Dillon assignee of "Sokley Dolson"; warrant 157 from John Adair's office; 400 ac on waters of Roaring R, in "Jaction" Co, begins at post oak marked "4 T H", runs W, S for complement where Richard Copeland lives; James Taylor locator ["Gossrd Erued" written in margin].

p. 31
78. Sept. 18, 1802 "Henery" Larns; military warrant 1440; 274 ac in "Jaction" Co on waters of Roaring R, begins at post oak on ridge of "rorieus land distance" S of a path from William Russell's to Bartholomew Donekins, runs N, E for complement, includes 3 small improvements "to wit" Bengam. Stewart's, widow Davis, & Mr. Cowanp [or Lowanp] and "land fit for cultivation", excluside of "pryer" claims; Thomas Dillon locator.

79. Sept. 18, 1802 Willoughby Williams, assignee of Simon Smith; military warrant 1321; 274 ac on dividing ridge between waters of Roaring R & waters of Flins Cr, runs near head of Doe Cr, a branch of Cumberland R, begins at chesnut marked "4 T", runs W, S, includes "said" improvement fit for cultivation, exclusive of pryer claims; James Taylor locator.

p. 32
80. Sept 18, 1802 James Hurtner; warrant 307 from John Adair's office; 250 ac in "Jaction" Co on waters of Roaring R, begins at black oak marked "W" at foot of a ridge, runs E, N for complement, includes improvement where Cornelis "Crorsly" lives; Thomas Dillon locator.

81. Sept. 18, 1802 Elijah Robertson; military warrant 9 as quarter master of guard appointed [for] commissioners; 624 ac in "Jaction" Co on waters of Roaring R, begins on E side of Lick Cr at dogwood & chesnut, runs W 260 poles crossing the creek to "P" chesnut, & N for complement; Thomas Dillon locator.

p. 33
82. Sept. 18, 1802 John Porterfield, assignee of "Frances" Owan; military warrant 221; 228 ac on N side of Cumberland R, on Jinnings Cr, begins at beach & sycamore, runs to include improvement made by Joseph Russell "or" to include improvement that "was" said Russell's Mar. 9, 1802 and "said" complement, exclusive of pryor claims; [no locator].

83. Sept. 18, 1802 John Gray Blount, assignee of heirs of Ben Sanders; balance of miliary warrant 5104 for 640 ac; 320 ac in Jackson Co on W fork of Roaring R; begins at 3 post oaks near path "comes" to Taylor's 320 ac tract, runs W, & N for complement; Thomas Dillon locator.

p. 34

84. Sept. 18, 1802 William Parson, assignee of heirs of Luke Turner; balance of military warrant 3383 for 640 ac; 320 ac in Jackson Co on waters of main fork of Roaring R, begins at large poplar & dogwood marked "O", runs N, & E for complement; Thomas Dillon locator; made void Oct. 10, 1802 by Thomas Dillon.

85. Sept 18, 1802 Edward "Harriss", assignee of Melordy Russell; balance of military warrant 637 for 640 ac; 320 ac in "Jaction" Co on branch of S fork of Roaring R, begins at 2 hickorys & a poplar, runs E, & S for complement; Thomas Dillon locator.

p. 35

86. [no date] John Morris, heir of "Ben"; balance of military warrant 1476; 320 ac in "Jaction" Co on head of eastern branch of Roaring R, begins on head of eastern branch of Roaring R at 2 large trees "ellam" & beach "standing near" with "many" letters, runs S, & W for complement; Thomas Dillon locator.

87. Sept. 18, 1802 heirs of William Hayes [Haynes on warrant]; balance of military warrant 39 for 320 ac; 320 ac in "Jaction" Co on main fork of Roaring R, begins at beech marked "T D" & sugar tree on S side of the river, uns W, & N for complement; Thomas Dillon locator.

p. 36

88. Sept. 18, 1802 William "Shephart" [Sheppard on warrant]; part of military warrant 3553 for 1,252 ac; 417 ac in Jackson Co, begins at 2 hickories on N side of a creek, runs E, & N for complement; Thomas Dillon locator.

89. Sept. 18, 1802 William Sheppard; balance of military warrant 3553 for 1,252 ac; 417 ac in Jackson Co, begins at 2 beaches & sugar tree on North of a creek, runs E, & S for complement; Thomas Dillon locator.

p. 37

90. Sept. 18, 1802 James "Poterfield", heir of Denoy [Demcy on warrant] Porterfield; part of warrant 100 for 3,840 ac; 1,280 [or 1,208] ac in "Jaction" Co, on middle fork of Roaring R, begins at black oak & white oak on N side of said fork, on a ridge, runs E, & S for complement; Thomas Dillon locator.

90A [no number]. (no date) James Poterfield, heir of "Denney" Porterfield; balance of military warrant 100 for 3,840 ac; 1,280 ac in Jackson Co on a branch of Roaring R, begins at black oak & white oak on N side of said fork on a ridge, runs E, & S for complement; this entry is not worded agreeable to location & it is moved to following page 38.

p. 38

91. Sept. 18, 1802 James Poterfield, heir of "Denney" Porterfield; balance of military warrant 100 for 3,840 ac; 1,280 ac in Jackson Co on a branch of Roaring R, begins at black oak & white oak on N side of said fork on a ridge, runs E, & S for complement; Thomas Dillon locator.

92. Oct. 2, 1802 John Stickley; military warrant 5203; 320 ac in Jackson Co, on waters of Roaring R, begins at a white oak marked "X" on top of a hill above mouth of Blackburns Br, runs E, & S for complement; Benjamin Blackburn locator "coppy erased".

p. 39
93. Oct. 8, 1802 David Harbert, assignee of Thomas Dillon; warrant [blank]; 400 ac in Jackson Co on "Dow" Cr, begins at an ash marked "H" being first creek that empties into Cumberland [R} below mouth of Roaring R; this entry made of military "guard" warrant [no number]; this entry is removed to page 47.

94. Oct. 8, 1802 "Christion" Rhodes; warrant 619; 640 ac in Jackson Co, on waters of middle fork of Roaring R, begins at 2 post oaks on line of 1,000 ac survey, runs N, E for complement, includes improvement of "Martain Dale a David Waldron"; Thomas Dillon locator.

p. 40
95. Oct. 8, 1802 Robert King, assignee of William Dobbin assignee of James McElloy; guard right warrant to Evans battalion; 400 ac in Jackson Co on N side of CumberlandcornerR, about 240 yards above mouth of Roaring R, at an elm & 2 sycamores on "Thomer's" line, runs with his line & up the river for complement; Thomas Dillon locator.

96. Oct. 8, 1802 Nathaniel Taylor assignee of Landon Carter; warrant 1112 from Carter's office for 100 ac dated Jan. 14, 1779 which was assigned by Landon Carter to Nathaniel Taylor; 100 ac in Jackson Co, begins at SW fork of Roaring R, "begins" at 2 white oaks on S bank of "said creek", runs down both sides of the creek for complement; Nathaniel "Tantor" locator, "coppy erased".

p. 41
97. Oct. 8, 1802 Nathaniel Taylor, assignee of David "Grnt"; military warrant 3741 for 640 ac to David Grant assigned to "Mayton" Thompson and assigned back to said Grant who assigned to Nathaniel Taylor and formerly entered by said Taylor in Jackson Co, and on surveying same he got "but" 250 ac as appears by surveyor's certificate dated Oct. 1, 1802; 150 ac in Jackson Co on Doe Cr of Cumberland R, begins below Noble's cabbin on W side of the creek "for complement", includes "cord" cabbin & Noble's cabbin; Nathaniel Taylor locaotor, "coppy erased".

98. Oct. 8, 1802 Jacob Work, assignee of William Wadlow; warrant 375 from

Adair's office by William Wadlow [or Wadloe] who transferred to said Work "being" Mar. 29, 1780; 100 ac in "Jaction" Co on head branch of Roaring R, includes plantation & improvement where William Bradley and his brother live; "coppy erased".

p. 42
99. Oct. 8, 1802 Jacob Work, assignee of William Rosebury; warrant 311 from Adair's office entered Mar. 16, 1780 by William Rosebery who assigned to said Work; 150 ac in Jackson Co on head of an eastern branch of Roaring R, begins nearly NE of where James Worthen lives at 2 beaches, runs "as law will admit" to include plantation & improvement where James Worthen lives; James Taylor locator.

100. Oct. 8, 1802 Jacob Work, assignee ofcornerMoses Looney; warrant 502 from Adair's office due to entry Apr. 20, 1780 by Moses Looney who sold to said Work; 600 ac in Jackson Co, on N fork of Roaring R, on waters of same, includes plantation where Mrs. Ledbetter's mill right is and Mr. Lins [or Hins] lives; James Taylor locator "coppy erased".

p. 43
101. Oct. 8, 1802 Abraham Taylor, assignee of Robert Lusk; warrant 1108 from Carter's office on entry Jan. 13, 1779 assigned "in favor" of Robert Lusk who assigned to Abraham Taylor; 200 ac in Jackson Co on waters of Roaring R, joins James Taylor's land, begins where said Taylor's [line] intersects "the Indion" line, runs with said Taylor's line, "according to law" for complement; Abraham Taylor locator.

102. Oct. 8, 1802 Nathaniel Taylor, assignee of David Grant assignee of Mayton Thompson assignee back to Nathaniel Taylor; military warrant 3761 for 640 ac dated Sept. 6, 1799 in favor of [David] Grant who transferred to Mayton Thompson and assigned back to said Grant who assigned to Nathaniel Taylor; 50 ac in Jackson Co on Blackburns Fork of Roaring R, begins at sycamore "seposed" to be corner of survey said to be made for Watson & supposed to be corner of 1,000 ac survey for "David", runs S, "so round", includes Thomas McGinson's improvement; formerly enters in "Jaction" Co and when surveyed was only 250 ac, then appearing 390 ac remaining of warrant due to said Taylor; "coppy erased"; Oct. 23, 1802 made void by order of James Taylor; [on p. 44:] unsatisfied 250 ac which said Taylor appears to be entitled to agreeable to law and "of" 250 ac said Taylor enters 50 ac as above located Oct. 8, 1802, Nathaniel Taylor locator.

p. 44
103. Oct. 8, 1802 Nathaniel Taylor, heir of James Taylor deceased; warrant 682 from Carter's office dated Dec. 9, 1778; 50 ac in Jackson Co, on waters of Roaring R, includes plantation & improvement where Cornelious "Crowlay" lives;

Nathaniel Taylor locator.

104. Oct. 8, 1802 Nathaniel Taylor, assignee of Isaac Taylor; warrant 2338 in Carter's office due to entry Dec. 10, 1779 by Isaac Taylor and assigned to Nathaniel Taylor; 640 ac for Nathaniel Taylor "& Abraham Taylor" in Jackson Co on waters of Mill Cr, branch of Cumberland R, includes 3 beaches marked "MIT" [or "MH"] and other letters at head of a spring; Nathaniel & Abraham Taylor locator, "coppy erased".

p. 45
105. Oct. 9, 1802 Nathaniel Taylor, assignee of John McNabb; warrant 40 from Carter's office due to entry Feb. 25, 1778 by John McNabb and transferred to said Taylor; 300 ac in Jackson Co, for Nathaniel Taylor "& Abraham Taylor", on head waters of Roaring R, begins at head of Doe Cr, runs down right hand fork of the creek, where "one" Joseph Taylor lives for complement; Joseph Taylor locator.

106. Oct. 9, 1802 Nathaniel Taylor, assignee of David Grant assignee of Mayton Thompson assignee back to Nathaniel Taylor; part of warrant 3761 dated Sept. 16, 1792 in favor of David Grant who transferred to Mayton Thompson who assigned back to said Grant who assigned to Nathaniel Taylor who is entitled to 190 ac of the warrant by certificate of entry taker; 50 ac in Jackson Co on S side of Cumberland R, between Garrott Fitzgerald & "Hennory" McKiney; James Taylor locator, "coppy erased".

p. 46
107. Oct. 16, 1802 Joseph Lock assignee of William Hart assignee of Josep. Loirs assignee of Mark "Fedwoods"; military warrant 1520 [or W20]; 640 ac on "a rathes" ford, begins on "Wanne's" upper corner on N side of Cumberland R, runs 200 poles up said line, & up the river for complement, includes where he lives; Joseph Lock locator.

108. Oct. 18, 1802 John Tally assignee of Garrot Fitzgerald assignee of Thomas Talton(maybe) of William Larson of Richson. Marshall of John Marshall of Jacob Farmer; [military] warrant 3383; 640 ac on S side of Doe Cr, near top of a ridge, beween Doe Cr & Flins Cr, begins at a chesnut oak marked "J H", runs S, includes John Horser's improvement, "said" complement, & runs "long" said ridge for complement; John Tally locator.

p. 47
109. Oct. 18, 1802 David Harbert assignee of Thomas Dillon; guart warrant [number blank]; 175 ac in Jackson Co, on "Rushghey" Fork of Flins Cr, begins at an ash marked "W", includes John Henser's improvement, includes said land fit for cultivation; David Harbert locator; Sept. 1, 1803 made void by order of David Harbert.

110. Oct. 22, 1802 Ephraim Payton assignee of Thomas Kenney; military warrant 156; 480 ac in Jackson Co, on S side of Cumberland R, begins in bend of the river where Thomas "Rmpson" lived "in an at a tree" marked "E P, runs to include the vacant land in said bent; Ephraim Payton locator.

p. 48
111. Oct. 25, 1802 Philip Coilter; warrant 54; 428 ac on N side of Cumberland R, joins Christopher Bullard's line on river bank, runs up the river for complement to said Bullard's E corner "to begin said" warrant granted to Phillip Britter; Abner Henley locator.

112. Oct. 25, 1802 Robert Carmichael; warrant 1; 640 ac on N side of Cumberland R, joins my other entry on N side, and joins Christopher Bullard's line, runs with said lines for complement; Abner "Hanley" locator; "Jun. 6" made void by Abner Hanley.

p. 49
113. Oct. 30, 1802 Levi Jarvis; military warrant 26 issued to Levi Jarvis, private in NC continental line; 226 ac in Jackson Co on Doe Cr that empties into Cumberland R below 640 ac entered by John Billingbey & Taylor, begins at a cabbin "partley rased against" mouth of a branch "or" near it, runs up & down for complement; David Cox locator.

114. Nov. 4, 1802 William Megee, assignee of James & John "Eveill" [or maybe Everitt] assignees of David Cobb; warrant 5103; 640 ac in Jackson Co, begins on William "Warter's" upper line on Roaring R, runs up said Roaring R to best advantage for complement; "Boz Burris" locator; "set" void by Boz Burris; "removed to following page 50".

p. 50
114A (no number & lined out). Nov. 12, 1802 Boz Burris assignee of James & John Everitt assignee of David "Joble"; Boz Burris, for William Megee; military warrant 5103; 640 ac in Jakson Co, on Roaring R; Boz Burris locator.

115. Nov. 12, 1802 Boz Burris assignee of James & John Everitt assignee of David "Joble"; Boz Burris, for William Megee; military warrant 5103; 640 ac in Jackson Co on Roaring R, on William Warter's W line, runs down Roaring R; Box Burris locator.

116. Nov. 15, 1802 James Taylor & "Hennery Weybourn" [or Weyburn], assignee of David Grant assignee of Motherial Thompson; military warrantcorner3761 dated Sept. 6, 1792 & assgned by David Grant to Nathaniel Taylor who assigned to James Taylor & "Hennary" Reybourn; 140 ac on E fork of Mill Cr, a branch of Cumberland R, begins at an oak marked "I T IL R" on S side of said E fork, runs as law will direct to include a buflow lick on said fork and "said" improvement;

Hennery Reyburn locator.

p. 51
117. Dec. 8, 1802 Uriah Anderson, assignee of Joseph Davis & of William Hart & Thomson Sarword & assignee of David Coulet; "guard right" warrant 4120 sold by Joseph Lock to said Anderson; 299 ac in Jackson Co on waters of Flins Cr & banch of Wallises Br, begins above cabbin & improvement where said Wallis lived, runs down the creek for complement; Uriah Anderson locator.

118. Jan. 6, 1803 Isaac Taylor, assignee of Samuel Johnson "per" wife Winney; [military] warrant 41; 640 ac in Jackson Co on main fork of Roaring R, joins 640 ac where Elijah Ewings lives, begins on S side of said river a beach marked "A D", runs as law will admit for complement, includes an improvement where said Ewings made corn last season, & joins said tract(sic); Isaac Taylor locator.

p. 52
119. Jan. 15, 1803 John McDonnold assignee of George Jorden; warrant 38; 100 ac on N side of Red R, joins John Hinds & James Mayberry 4,400 [may be shuck 219 in Middle Dist in NC grants to John "Hynds" & "Francis" Mayberry] ac tract, begins at NE corner sugar tree marked "I M I M" (sic), runs N, S, E, making long side North & side; John McDonnold locator "revoved to page".

120. Feb. 2, 1803 David Chester; part of warrant 57 for 1,000 ac issued Feb. 2, 1803 to said David Chester, sergeant in late continental line; 250 ac in Jackson Co on Trace Cr on N side of Christopher "Bullar" 640 ac survey & Abner Henley's 428 ac survey "if required" & William Robertson "if required", "joins them", runs up & down Trace Cr and with said lines before mentioned, includes "vaneansey" as may be required; Abner Hanley locator.

p. 53
121. Feb. 2, 1803 David Chester; military warrant 57 issued Nov. 19, 1802 to David Chester, sergeant in late continental line; 500 ac in Jackson Co on N side of Cumberland R, at mouth of Cube [or Lube] Cr, on the river below mouth of said creek, about mouth of said creek, runs up & down the river & creek for complement as may be required; Abner Hanley locator.

122. Feb. 2, 1803 David Chester; part of military warrant 57 for 1,000 ac issued Nov. 19, 1802 to David Chester for his services as sergeant in late continental line; 250 ac in Jackson Co on "Cob" Cr "where or" includes improvement of James Simson & Skags at the big springs, Greenhoe's imrovement, runs up & down Cob Cr, & joins "it"; Abner Hanley locator.

p. 54
123. Feb. 4, 1803 James S Ganes & William McCutchin [or McCritchin], claiments of Gidden Harris & William "Nelston"; warrants 1233 for 640 ac and

208 for 380 ac; 1,029 ac in Jackson Co, on main N fork of Roaring R, begins where Obed Road crosses said river "supposed" to be 0.25 miles below fork of Red R, runs up the river on both sides of both forks for complement; James S "Gains" locator.

124. Feb. 17, 1803 Nathaniel Venable, claiment of "Joabb" [Jacob in entry book] Chamberlin; warrant 798 from Carter's office issued May 1, 1779; 200 ac in Jackson Co on Coplins Fork of Roaring R, joins Joseph "Coaplaind's" 400 ac entry; "Mar. 5" made void by order of William Chohethers(maybe, faint).

p. 55
125. Feb. 17, 1803 Nathaniel Taylor, claiment of Thomas Mitchel; warrant 2464 from Carter's office dated Mar. 15, 1778; 100 ac in Jackson Co on waters of Roaring R, joins Joseph Coopland's 400 ac entry on N side, runs to include a sinking spring; [blank], locator "copy erased".

126. Feb. 17, 1803 William McCutchin, claimant of Timothey Holdaway; warrant 765 from Carter's office dated "Way" 2, 1799; 100 ac on waters of Coaplands Fork of Roaring R, begins at or near Obed Road, abou 200 yards W of a large spring known as Trouble Spring, runs to include said spring; William McCutchin [or Millihan] locator.

p. 56
127. Feb. 17, 1803 Nathaniel Taylor; warrant 2122 from Carter's office dated Oct. 13, 1780; 100 ac in Jackson Co on waters of Spring Cr, branch of Roaring R, begins at beginning corner post oak & black [oak] of John Rice's grant standing on S side of the creek & on a bluff nearly West of where Eligah Chisholm lives, runs E with said line, & S for complement; William Mechloh(maybe), locator, "coppy erased".

128. Feb. 17, 1803 William McCutchen, claiment of Joab "Michaell"; warrant 1359 from Carter's office dated Oct. 26, 1779; 100 ac in Jackson Co on Spring Cr, joins Rice on East; William McCutchen locator "coppy erased".

p. 57
129. Feb. 17, 1803 James Stuart, claimant of George Adams; warrant 1963 from Carter's office dated Feb. 15, 1781; 150 ac in Jackson Co on waters of Roaring R, begins at or near a path from Peter Huston's to Isaac Bullard's, runs to includes improvement made by George Tolley; William McCutchen locator "coppy erased".

130. Feb. 26, 1803 heirs of Christopher Lackey; [military] warrant 65; 2,560 ac in Jackson Co on S side of Cumberland R, in bent where Thomas Simpson lives, begins on river bank near where James Rattly lives, runs down the river for complement; Abner Stubblefield locator; made void "Aug. 27" by A Stubblefield.

first p. 58
131. Feb, 27, 1803 Garrott Fitzgerald [other names smudged]; warrant 4701; 640 ac on N side of William "Harress" Cr, on a little branch running to said creek waters of Brimstone [Cr], begins at dogwood marked "I C", runs down the creek & as law directs, includes a small lick on said branch about 0.5 miles below Harris where "he" lives; Jabaz Fitzgerald locator.

132. Mar. 3, 1803 Benjamin Blackburn; military warrant 5203; 285 ac in Jackson on waters of Roaring R, begins at a post oak marked "X" and "dimond" below the cross, runs W, N for complement; Benjamin Blackburn locator.

second p. 58
132A (number blank). Mar. 7, 1803 Nathaniel Taylor & William "McCuthan"; warrants 73 and 361 from Adair's "Elis" Gains' office for 640 ac each; 1,240 ac in Jackson Co on Coaplins Fork of Roaring R, joins Indian boundary line, Joseph Coaplin's 400 ac entry, runs with "said" for complement; this location "sot" in the book "rong" & is right on page 59 [number 134].

133. Mar. 6, 1803 Edmond "Tinnons"; warrant [or "subbleat"] 2320; 191 ac on Dry Fork of Flins Cr, includes vacant land between Samson Williams & Sturthers "and also" Job Anderson; Edmond Tinnons locator.

p. 59
134. Mar. 7, 1803 Nathaniel Taylor & William McCutchen; warrants 73 and 361 from Adair's "Elis" Gains' office for 640 ac each; 1,240 ac in Jackson Co on Coaplins Fork of Roaring R, joins Indian boundary line, Joseph Coplin's 400 ac entry, runs with "said" for complement; William McCuthchen locator "coppy erased".

135. Mar. 7, 1803 Nathaniel McNabb, claiment of John Forgeson; warrant 524 from Carter's office dated Oct. 22, 1778; 300 ac in Jackson Co on waters of Spring Cr, joins James Taylor's land where he lives, runs to include place known as Poke Patch; [no locator] "coppy erased".

p. 60
136. Mar. 7, 1803 Andrew Reed; warrant 553 from Carter's office dated Mar. 26, 1779; 400 ac in Jackson Co on Flins Cr, branch of Cumberland R, begins at a beach marked "WMG 1803" standing on N side of waggon road, nearly opposite mouth of a fork of said creek known as Rush Fork, runs down both sides of the creek for complement; [no locator].

137. Mar. 8, 1803 John McDonnold; warrant 38; 100 ac on N side of Wolf R, joins John Hinds & Francis Mayberry's 4,400 ac tract, begins at NE corner sugar tree & beech marked "+ M + M" (sic), runs N, S, E, & W, includes vacant land

between other lines; John McDonnold locator.

p. 61
138. Mar. 16, 1803 James Mayberry; warrant 6; 74 ac on N side of Wolf R, begins at 2 dogwoods marked [backward "S H"] standing on small ridge between Lewis Harris & Fisgarrot's improvement, runs E 80 poles, S 150]poles], W 80 poles, N 150 poles to beginning, includes improvement of said Fitsgarrot; [no locator].

139. Mar. 26, 1803 Benjamin Poor, [name smudged]; warrant 4; 100 ac in Jackson Co on waters of Wolf R, begins at black oak & 2 dogwoods, runs S, W, includes "the" improvement for complement; Benjamin Poor locator.

p. 62
140. Apr. 2, 1803 John Swain & Armst. Stubblefield, assignees "originally" of Luke Lamb Terril deceased & administrator of said heirs; warrant 3018; 2,560 ac in Jackson Co on head waters of Brimstone Cr, begins 0.5 miles below small "palth" lick, runs up the creek, & includes lick and 2 "bank" of iron ore; John Swain & Armsterd Stubblefield locators.

141. Apr. 21, 1803 William McNabb, assignee of Mary Hall; warrant 2103 from Carter's office; 100 ac in Jackson Co on W fork of Russells Mill Cr, on which fork William Prior lives, begins at post oak on E side of said creek, on "a large" marked "WMCC", runs as law directs for complement; Isaac Taylor locator.

p. 63
142. Apr. 21, 1803 John "Craford" assignee of John "Aksier"; warrant 305 from Adair's ofice; 100 ac in Jackson Co on Roaring R, on mouth of Lick Cr, begins at a beach at large tree "reard", includes spring & improvement of William Harkle "now lives"; [no locator] "copp erased".

143. Apr. 22, 1803 Benjamin Lockhart, claiment of Joseph Tucker; warrant 2316 from Carter's office issued "in favor" of Joseph Tucker; 50 ac in Jackson Co on Eagle Cr, branch of Obed R, begins "in" fork of said creek at 2 post oaks nearly E of where Benjamin "Poton" lives, runs according to law for complement, includes improvement where Benjamin Tallon lives; [no locator].

p. 64
144. Apr. 23, 1803 John Williams, claiment "under" Obediah Hammonds; warrant 72; 150 ac in Jackson Co on waters of Wolf R known as Dry Cr, includes place where said Williams lives, begins at black oak & dogwood marked "I W", runs "each way" for complement, includes all land fit for cultivation in said bounds; "Hennory" Rowan locator.

145. Apr. 23, 1803 John Carter, claiment of Micajah Thomas; [Carter] warrant 2497; 600 ac in Jackson Co, on both sides of Eagle Cr waters of Obeds R, includes

an improvement made by "Alexandry Just", begins 250 poles East of beginning of said Carter & McNutty's 3,000 ac grant, runs N with their line, E, S to beginning; Hennory Rowan locator; set void "Aug. 8" by order of John Carter.

p. 65
146. Apr. 23, 1803 Hennary Rowan, claiment of Micajah Thomas, I transfer this entry to William Hill for value received of him Henry Rowan; warrant 2497 from Armstrong's office; 400 ac in Jackson Co on both sides of waggon roa from Long Bottom on Obeds R to Harrecane Hill, known as Parris Spring place, where William Mill now lives; Hennory Rowan locator; transferred Mar. 12, 1804, original warrant "lifed void tow" annext No. 303 (sic).

147. Apr. 23, 1803 Conrod Peters, claiment of William McCormack; warrant 303 from Adair's office; 320 ac in Jackson Co on both sides of "Kany" Fork of Wolf R, includes place where "said" Files lives, runs agreeable to survey (sic); Hennory Rowan locator.

p. 66
148. Apr. 23, 1803 Hennory Rowan, claiment of William McCormack; warrant 303 from Adair's office; 320 ac in Jackson Co on Kany Fork of Wolf R, includes place where Samuel Blair lives, runs agreeable to survey (sic); Hennory "Rowen" locator.

149. Apr. 23, 1803 "Henory" Rowan, claiment of "Dannal" Yeats; warrant 175 from Carter's office; 150 ac in Jackson Co on N side of Obeds R, opposite & below mouth of Eagle Cr, near John "Uzlron" line, known as "Hors shew" Bottom, runs on meanders of the river for complement; Hennory Rowen locator.

p. 67
150. Apr. 23, 1803 John Lee, claiment of "Dannol" Yeats; warrant 175 from Carter's office; 50 ac in Jackson Co on both sides of Kany Fork of Wolf R, includes an improvement made by himself, begins at sugar tree & poplar marked "‡‡", runs "each" way for complement, includes all land fit for cultivation in said bounds; Hennery Rowen locator.

151. Apr. 30, 1803 Moses Fisk, assignee of Stokley "Donlson" assignee of Benjamin Thomas; warrant 4132; 640 ac in Jackson Co, between Roaring R & waters of Mill Cr, begins at white oak & red oak marked "F" and "3" standing about 110 poles W of NW corner of Samuel Sanford's grant that includes plantation where Andrew "McCare" lives, runs N to 60,400 ac grant to said Donelson [maybe shuck 508 in Eastern Dist, in NC grants], E to join said Sanford's said tract "jand granted" to Benjamin "Shepard"; Moses Fisk locator.

page 68
152. May 6, 1803 Willie Cherry, assignee of "Elizebeth" Mchoon heir of Ralph

Mchoon; warrant 5110 [used for Tennessee grants in Jackson Co & Wilson Co see item 8593 in book on military warrants]; 25 ac in Jackson Co on first large branch that crosses Walton's Road above said "William" Cherry's house that is "on" said road, supposed to be 2 or 3 miles from said Cherry's improvement, at Cub Run, joins Indian boundary line of N, near where it crosses said branch, on W side of said branch, runs "down & up" the branch on both sides for complement; Willie Cherry locator.

153. May 6, 1803 Willie Cherry, assignee of Elizebeth Mchoon heir of Ralph Mchoon; warrant 5110; 400 ac in Jackson Co, on dividing ridge between "big Barn" [maybe big Barron R] & on head waters of Jenings Cr, joins survey granted to David Langston, assignee of Caleb McTarshen's heirs on warrant 2676 [Sumner Co 470, heir of Caleb "McFashion"], on W & S of said survey, runs as law directs for complement; Willie Cherry locator.

p. 69
154. May 11 1803 Moses Fisk, assignee of Howel Tatum, warrant 118 issued by William "Maclain", Tennessee Secretary of State; 100 ac in Jackson Co southerly from Sampsons Fork of Miller Cr, westerly of place where John Black lines, runs to include improvement and spring where widow Black & Samuel McCown live occupied last year by John Hutcheson jr; (no locator).

155. May 11, 1802 Moses Fisk; warrant 189 [118 also mentioned] issued by William Maclin, Tennessee Secretary of State; 567 ac in Jackson Co on waters of Roaring R, begins at 7 white oaks & several dogwoods on "a rive" SW of path from old Mr. "Offiers" to John Mitchell's, runs W 108 poles, N 330 poles to large sweet gum, poplar, elm & dogwood standing above said Mitchell's upper spring, & E for quantity; Moses Fisk locator.

p. 70
156. May 11, 1803 Moses Fisk; warrant 190 issued by William Maclin Secretary of State of Tennessee; 260 ac in Jackson Co, West of grant to Samuel Sanford that includes plantation where Andrew McClaine lives, begins at beech, 2 poplars & 3 hickories on side of a hill about 20 poles S of NW corner of said tract granted to Sanford, runs W, & S for quantity; Moses Fisk locator.

157. May 11, 1803 Moses Fisk; warrant 191 issued by William Maclin Secretary of State of Tennessee; 100 ac in Jackson Co on waters of Roaring R, south westerly from Capt. Mitchell's, easterly of Coperas Cr, begins 30 poles W of 2 dead hickories & dogwood which were marked as SE corner of 180 ac "measured off" for said Mitchell where he lives, and 160 poles S of large sweet gum standing near his upper spring to run W, N, & S for complement; Moses Fisk locator.

p. 71
158. May 11, 1803 Moses Fisk; warrant 192 issued by William Maclin Secretary

of State of Tennessee; 100 ac in Jackson Co on waters of Roaring R, begins at 7 white oaks and several dogwoods standing on a rise south westerly of path from old Mr. "Offisers" to Capt. Mitchell's, being beginning of said Fisk's entry on warrant 189, runs E, & S for quantity; Moses Fisk locator.

159. May 11, 1803 Moses Fisk; warrant 194 issued by William Maclin Secretary of State of Tennessee; 50 ac in Jackson Co on road from one of said Fisk's fields to Elijah Ewing's, on each side of said road, north westerly from Capt. Mitchell's, includes an old camp near where the path that passes from said Mitchell's by his upper spring joins said road; Moses Fisk locator.

page 72
160. May 11, 1803 M Maclison Fisk, assignee of Moses Fisk assignee of James T Gains; supernumery warrant 16; 200 ac in Jackson Co on waters of Roaring R, begins at 7 white oaks & several dogwoods on a rise south westerly of path from old Mr "Officers" to Capt. Mitchell's corner of one or 2 locations of said Moses Fisk, runs S, & W for quantity; Moses Fisk locator.

161. May 17, 1803 Georg. Geer [James May, inserted] assignee of John Amis assignee of William Roberts; warrant 72; 250 ac in Jackson Co on Blackburns Fork of Roaring R, begins at an ash "vsermet" & which oak is Thomas Williams corner on E side of said fork, on "rockkay pont", runs to include plantation where said Geer lives, includes both sides of the creek for complement; George Geer locator.

p. 73
162. May 17, 1803 James Williams, assignee of William Sturt; warrant 351; 150 ac in Jackson Co on Blackburns Fork of Roaring R, begins at an "ash warrent" & white oak on E side of said fork, on a "rockkey pint", runs S up the creek, includes both sides of the creek and plantation where said Williams lives for complement; George Greer locator.

163. May 26, 1803 William T Lewis, assignee of Stokley Donelson & Alexander Cotter; military warrant 5174; 640 ac in Jackson Co, between Roaring R and Sampsons Fork of Mill Cr with place which John Black got of George Hutcheson, begins at a sourwood, white oak & poplar 200 poles S of NW corner of Moses Fisk's entry that includes improvement & claim "sold as aforesaid" by said Hutcheson to Black, runs E, & S for quantity; Moses Fisk locator.

p. 74
164. May 26, 1803 Moses Fisk, assignee of Samuel Jackson; military warrant 211 signed by William Macalin (sic); 50 ac in Jackson Co on waters of Sampsons Fork on N side, joins his entry he got of George Hutcheson, begins at a beech near a branch, about 0.5 miles E of beginning corner of said Fisk's former entry, runs W, N, & E for quantity; Moses Fisk locator.

165. May 26, 1803 Moses Fisk, assignee of Samuel Jackson; military warrant 210 "signed" by William Maclin; 100 ac in Jackson Co "surtherly" of place where widow Black lives, begins at poplar & dogwood "some" distance to right of "near" road passing by John Black's towards Elijah "Eweing", about 0.5 miles W of NW corner of entry made today for William T Lewis said Fisk locates, location No. 165 (sic, maybe 163) warrant 5174, runs W, S, E for quantity to include large spring & cane land; Moses Fisk locator.

p. 75
166. May 27, 1803 Moses Fisk; warrant 317 signed by William Maclin; 230 ac in Jackson Co on road which goes along the ridge between waters of Roaring R & Sinking and Sampson Forks of Mill Cr, begins at corner white oak & red oak marked "F" of another location of said Fisk's, about 110 poles W of NW corner of grant to Samuel Sanford that includes Andrew McLane's plantation, runs N to "the" big tract granted to Stokley Donelson in 1795, & W for quantity; Moses Fisk locator.

167. Jun. 11, 1803 Thomas Elliott, assignee of Joel Kiser; warrant 2287; 200 ac in Jackson Co on W side of Eagle Cr, includes place where Jacob Meeks lives, being improvement made by Eutus Grigg, runs each way for complement; Thomas Elliott locator.

p. 76
168. Jun. 20, 1803 Moses Fisk; warrant 326 "signed" by William Maclin; 100 ac in Jackson Co, on waters of Coperas Cr, S of location for John & Robert Allen on warrant 4328 location No. 44 entered Jul. 9, 1802, this location to begin 25 poles S of poplar & black gum marked as Allen's SW corner by said Fisk "present" Messes "Bengerman" & Jackson, runs E, & S for quantity; Moses Fisk locator.

169. Jun. 20, 1803 Moses Fisk, assignee of Stokley Donelson assignee of James Chissum; military warrant 3954; 640 ac between Roaring R & Sampsons Fork of Mill Cr, begins 30 poles E of SE corner of his enty on warrant 3960 location 45 entered Jul. 26, 1802, runs N, S, & E for quantity; Moses Fisk locator.

p. 77
170. Jun. 20, 1803 Moses Fisk, assignee of James Harris(maybe); warrant 16; 200 ac on waters of Coperas Cr, begins 20 poles W of poplar & black gum marked as SW corner of John & Robert allen's location present Bingerman & two "Jacksons", runs S, N, W for quantity, includes white oak, 3 beeches & 3 small poplars marked "E" standing at or near head of a hollow of NW fork which comes into said Coperas Cr "caseoder"; Moses Fisk locator.

171. Jun. 21, 1803 William Robertson, assignee of Thomas Dillon(maybe) assignee of Isaac McDewel; [military] warrant 3937; 640 ac on N side of

Cumberland R, on Bullards Cr, begins at beach marked "W R" near fork of said creek, runs up & down the creek for complement, includes John Lee's improvement & Andrew Blackwood's improvement where he lives, and said Robertson's improvement; William Robertson locator; Jul. 29, 1806 I transfer 100 ac of above warrant & entry to Andrew Blackwood, 100 ac to John Lee, 240 ac to Jonas Bedford without recourse on me (signed) William "Roberson".

p. 78
172. Jun. 23, 1803 James Oar; warrant 658 from John Armstrong's office dated Jun. 24, 1784 "or so much as may be in following bounds"; 2,000 ac in Jackson Co, begins at double black oak marked "I O" amongst pointers on James Mayben's line of 5,000 ac, runs W with said line until it intersects "Hennary" Rowen's 330 ac survey, easterly with conditional line, includes Alexander A Kemons improvement, & westerly to beginning; James Oar locator.

173. Jun. 23, 1803 John Chisum sr, assignee of Elijah Chisum; warrant 742 dated Feb. 12, 1781 from John Adair's office "now kept" by James Gains esq; 50 ac in Jackson Co on Roaring R, begins at a beech about 30 poles below head of a large spring, runs up both sides of the river for complement, includes plantation where "or gsam this m Chisum lives"; James Oar locator.

p. 79
174. Jun. 13, 1803 Elijah Chisum; warrant 564 dated May 16, 1780 by John Adair's office now kept by James Gains; 170 ac in Jackson Co, begins at black oak marked "E C" on a bluff of Spring Cr, runs (blank), then East for complement, includes said Chisum's improvement where he lives; James "Ore" locator; made void by consent Jun. 13, 1805.

175. Jun. 27, 1803 William McCutchen & Isaac Taylor, claiments of Joshua Thompson; warrant 2496 for 50 ac from Carter's office dated Dec. 27, 1791; 50 ac in Jackson Co on S fork of Roaring R, joins James Blackburn's entry on East and Nathaniel Taylor's entry on North, said 50 ac to lye "cheafly" on E side of said creek; Isaac Taylor locator; made void by order of Isaac Taylor Jun. 3, 1804.

p. 80
176. Jun. 27, 1803 William "McCuten" & Isaac Taylor, claiments of John Shelby; warrant 92 for 200 ac from Carter's office issued Oct. 19, 1778; 200 ac in Jackson Co, on waters of Spring Cr, a fork of Roaring R, begins on "Indion" line nearly East of SE corner of Nathaniel Taylor's 50 ac survey that includes Cornelius Crowly's improvement, runs W to Taylor's line, with the Indion boundary line for complement; Isaac Taylor locator; made void Jun. 3, 1804 by order of Isaac Taylor.

177. Jun. 27, 1803 William McCutchen & Isaac Taylor, claiments of John Gillihan; warrant 2686 for 200 ac from Carter's office issued Mar. 29, 1782; 200

ac in Jackson Co on middle fork of Roaring R, begins at a spruce pine marked "HC" & ironwood saplin standing on river bank being corner of John "Crofford" sr's 833 ac tract; Isaac Taylor locator.

p. 81
178. Jun. 28, 1803 John Fitzgerald, assignee of James Easten attorney of heirs of William Corben; military warrant 4711 issued to heirs of William Corben assigned by James Easten attorney of said heirs; 640 ac in Jackson Co on N side of Cumberland R, begins on Jinnor's Cr at sugar tree & beech on "Ephrem" Payton's & Pret's S boundary line, runs down both sides of said creek, includes vacant land on said creek; Jun. 28, 1803 I certify above location was legally proved before me one of justices of peace of Jackson Co "Henary" McKinney location; location sold by James Fitzgerald to Abner Lee; date of transfer is Sept. 29 1803 (witness) David Lance.

179. Jul. 5, 1803 James Oar [or Ore]; due to balance of 2,000 ac in warrant 658 issued Jun. 24, 1784 from John Armstrong's office "for western land" entered by [blank, James Allen in entry book]; 500 ac in Jackson Co, begins at beech marked "I O" amongst poynters, runs W 200 poles, N 400 poles to include 2 fields & large sinking spring on head of "Egle" Cr where Jacob Coons lives; James Ore locator.

p. 82
180. Jul. 5, 1803 James Ore; balance (sic) of 2,000 ac in warrant 658 from John Armstrong's office "for western land"; 122 ac in Jackson Co, begins at a beech marked "I O" on bank of Obeds R, runs N10E 46 poles, E 10 poles to conditional line with William Sinclare, N24E 124 poles, N44W 88 poles, S65W 100 poles, S20E 80 poles, S17W 96 poles, & to beginning; James Ore locator.

181. Jul. 5, 1803 James Ore; balance (sic) of warrant 658 issued Jun. 24, 1784 from John Armstrong's office "for western land"; 295 ac in Jackson Co, begins at "mapole" marked "I O" on head of Nathaniel Caregers Cr, on "Indioin" boundary line, runs 80 poles with said line, N 218 poles, W 60 poles, S 20 poles, W 74 poles, S 59 poles, W 80 poles, S 159 poles, to beginning; James Ore locator.

p. 83
182. Jul. 5, 1803 Robert Glinn [or Linn], assignee of Elijah Eisum; warrant 43 dated Oct. 22, 1802 from William Maclin, Secretary of State; 50 ac, joins Samuel Landford's 640 ac survey where William "Rusell" lives, begins at black oak & poynters marked "R G", runs W to "Arbndish" Ore's line of William Rusel's mill tract, S to include said Glavens Spring & improvement; James "Oar" locator.

183. Jul. 7, 1803 James Herser [or Kerser], assignee originally of Hugh Forkpack(maybe); warrant (blank); 400 ac on Lick Cr waters of Roaring R, includes improvement where he lives and improvement where Powell formerly lived; James "Officer" locator.

184. Jul. 14, 1803 Jembes Corzin(maybe & Elijah Hisser(maybe); warrant 44; 50 ac, begins at black gum & white oak marked "B C" on S side of Copland Cr near E corner of Stephen Coat land, runs N, W, S, includes cane spring, includes house & land on both sides of the creek; Stephen Copland locator; transferred Jun. 13, 1805 (not signed).

p. 84
185. Jul. 21, 1803 Uriah Anderson, assignee of Thomas Dillon; [military] warrant 2885; 640 ac on main waggon road between old Mr. Henson & Wren's [or Wvens] cabbin, begins about 250 yards "of" said cabbin, begins at a red oak standing on lef hand of the road, runs southwardly, easterly, "so round" to include said cabbin, spring, improvement, & "said" complement; Uriah Anderson locator; Aug. 25, 1803 this entry void by "visble" order of Uriah Anderson.

186. Jul. 26, 1803 Garret Fitzgerrald, assignee of Charles Poore; military warrant 4338; 640 ac in Jackson Co, begins at foot of herricain ridge on a small branch of "Dowe" Cr, runs down both sides of said branch for complement, includes Isom's Spring & improvement where old Mr. Deel lived;]no locator]; made void Nov. 8, 1804 by order of "Garrot" Fitzgerrald.

p. 85
187. Aug. 2, 1803 Moses Fisk, assignee of Stockley Donelson of heirs of James R Whitney; military warrant 3960; 640 ac; entered Jul. 26, 1802 [location 45] alters said location to begin "as before" 120 poles S of 13 mile tree "therein alluded" to namely a hickory, beech & sugar tree, runs N 100 poles, E as before "intred" 282 poles, S as before, includes as before place where George Huckeson then lived & John Black lives now, S boundary will be on line of W T Lewis' tract 200 poles S of beginning first mentioned, beginning corner of Lewis' entry is sourwood, white oak & poplar; Moses Fisk locator.

188. Aug. 2, 1803 Moses Fisk, assignee of James Gaines; warrant 16 [maybe in Adair's office]; 200 ac on waters of Roaring R, SW of old Mr. "Offircer's", S of tract entered in name of "M Madison" Fisk which begins at 7 white oaks & several dogwoods, joins said tract, runs from its SW corner E, S, & "a little" W for quantity; Moses Fisk locator.

p. 86
189. Aug. 2, 1803 Moses Fisk, assignee of Samuel Jackson; warrant 211; 50 ac in Jackson Co, W of his entry where Samuel McCown lives, E of entry in name of William T Lewis, S of "the" big tract but not joining either, includes a spring & a flat of good land, begins at 2 dogwoods, runs N, & W; Moses Fisk locator.

190. Aug. 3, 1803 Nathaniel Taylor, assignee of Thomas Roe; warrant 201 from Carter's office issued Jan. 11, 1796; 200 ac in Jackson Co on Copelands Cr of

Roaring R, begins at NE corner 2 spanish oaks of Nathaniel Taylor's 100 ac survey standing on or near line of Josep. "Coopland's" 400 ac survey, runs W with Taylor's line, includes Walter Alley's improvement where Lenon lives, agreeable to law for complement, exclusive of pryor entries & claims; Isaac Taylor locator.

p. 87
191. Aug. 9, 1803 William Robertson; warrant 2937; 200 ac on N side of Cumberland R, on Bullards Cr, begins at sugar tree marked "W R" on E side of the creek, runs up & down the creek for complement, includes a large spring & improvement which said Robertson made; William Robertson locator.

192. Aug. 11, 1803 heirs of William Rhodes; [military] warrant 3285; 1,000 ac on N side of Cumberland R, "a few" miles below mouth of "Oby" R, begins at mouth of Dry Cr, runs up Cumberland [R], & off for complement; Moses Fisk locator; "Sept. 3" made void by order of Moses Fisk.

p. 88
193. Sept. 2, 1803 Amoter Stubblefield & Hennory "W" Lawson, assignees of heirs of Jeffey Davis; warrant 2808; 640 ac in Jackson Co, on Roaring R, begins at upper end of "Eweing's" tract, runs up both sides for quantity; Amoter Stubblefield & "Hennary" Lawson locators, "Aasterd" Stubblefield; May 9, 1805 I transfer above entry to Armstread Stubblefield by order of Hennary W Lawson (signed) John Fitzgerrald; reentered Dec. 3, 1809 in name of A Stubblefield.

194. Sept. 2, 1803 heirs of Christopher Lackey; [military] warrant 65; 2,560 ac in Jackson Co on both sides of Cumberland R, begins on Coner's upper line of 1,07 ac, runs up the river on N side, crosses, & runs down South side; A Stubblefield locator; Jun. 2, 1807 made void by W Slade, attorney & agent of heirs of Christopher Lackey (witness) "W C".

p. 89
195. Sept. 15, 1803 Elijah Chisum sr, assignee of James (smudge); [military] warrant 85; 320 ac in Jackson Co on Roaring R, begins a 2 beach trees one marked "B" & other marked "E C", runs down both sides of the river for complement, takes in Isaac Ogdon's claim & improvement and Thomas Boon's claim & improvement, "dun" by consent of each party; Elijah Chisum locator; Jun. 13, 1805 transferred to William Chisum.

196. Sept. 15, 1803 Elijah Chisum; [military] warrant 49; 100 ac in Jackson Co, on NE of & joins his former 170 ac entry where said Chisum lives; Elijah Chisum locator; Jun. 13, 1805 made void by consent (not signed).

p. 90
197. Sept. 15, 1803 Elijah Chisum sr; warrant 467; 170 ac in Jackson Co between

Robert Prentis' cabbin & Isaac Ogdon's "bry" [or big] "Landfield", includes white oak & "alam" spring, same land known as Boon's purchase from Prentis; Elijah Chisum locator; Jun. 13, 1805 made void by consent (not signed).

198. Sept. 15, 1803 Elijah Chisum; warrant 741; 150 ac in Jackson Co, includes cabbin that one Stout built on said Chisum's improvement, known as Sycamore Spring, runs to "the points" oblong for complement; Elijah Chisum locator; Jun. 13, 1805 made void by consent (not signed).

p. 91
199. Sept. 16, 1803 [Wm Moleston assignee Francis Maybury--lined out] "Simond" Huddleston sr & Francis Maybury; warrants 354 & 346; 30 ac in Jackson Co, begins on "Mabury's" & Hineses NW corner on N side of Wolf R, runs E 62 poles with said line, N 60 poles, W 150 [poles], S, & E for quantity; Francis Mabury & Simond Huddleston locators; "coppy erased", (no date) Simond Hudleston warrant is assigned to Francis Maybury by order "in name of" Maybury.

200. Sept. 16, 1803 Simon Huddleston assignee of Thomas Jackson; warrant 162; 160 ac, begins at W end of Huddleston's Cove on James Mabery's line about 3 "outs" from his NW corner, runs N to James Mabin sr's line, E between the 2 lines for quantity; Simond Huddleston locator.

p. 92
201. missing 202. missing

p. 93
203. missing

p. 94
204. Sept. 16, 1803 Stephen Mayfield, assignee of Elijah Chisum assignee of [blank]; warrants 51 & 48 signed by William Maclin, 48 is assigned to William Richardson and transferred back to Elijah Chisum then signed from Chisum to Stephen Mayfield, 51 is assigned by Chisum to Mayfield; 200 ac in Jackson Co on waters of Roaring R, begins at black oak, runs North & South to include "the" big pond cove and said Mayfield's Spring & improvement; Stephen Mayfield locator.

p. 94 & 95
205. Sept. 27, 1803 Samuel Moore, assignee of George Gordon; warrant 40 from "Macklin's" office assignee of George Gordon, "located" Sept. 25, 1803 (sic); 50 ac in Jackson Co on N side of W fork of Russells Mill Cr, begins at white oak marked (smudge, maybe "I M") sanding on conditional line made by Joseph Pryor & Enock Odle to be line between them, near a small hollow & path from said Odle to said Pryor's, runs to include improvement where said Odle lives and said

complement, agreeable to law; Samuel Moore locator; this entry transferred by order of Samuel Moore to John Starky.

p. 95
206. Sept. 27, 1803 Nathaniel Taylor; warrant 220 from Adair's office issued Feb. 21, 1788; 640 ac in Jackson Co on W fork of Flat Cr on which William Thompson lives, begins "a small" distance above where said Thompson lives, runs according to law to include said Thompson's improvement and where William Ballow "the trunk maker" lives, "an" "Hennary" Raybourn, & said complement, exclusive of pryor claims; Isaac Taylor locator.

207. Oct. 3, 1803 Elexander Coock; warrant 2539 from Carter's office; 200 ac in Jackson Co, begins at a white oak on N side of Flat Cr below "the" big falls, runs up the creek for complement, includes his spring & improvement; Elexander Coock locator; Jul. 12, (smudge) sold by Elexander Coock to James Taylor & George Taylor.

p. 96
208. Oct. 6, 1803 William Bradley, assignee of George Gordon; warrant 39 issued "by William Smoel assignee" of George Gordon; 10 ac in Jackson Co, begins at a black oak, runs SW, then northerly, "so round" to include said Bradley's Spring & improvement; William Bradley locator.

209. Oct. 6, 1803 Robert "Price", assignee of John Tally; [military] warrant 3383; 344.25 ac in Jackson Co, begins at a little beech marked "R P" on W side of Uriah Anderson's West line on a ridge, runs N to Fitzgerrald's line, along said line to Thompson's, & along Anderson's line to beginning; Robert Prise locator, entered on a certificate.

p. 97
210. Oct. 17, 1803 Uriah Anderson, assignee of Henry W Lawson assignee of (blank) Pursum assignee of Rodham Horne; military warrant 5157; 640 ac in Jackson Co, on head of Dry Fork of Flins Cr, begins at large poplar, runs "a little" West, then East, then down the creek to include "Jamens" Foxe's Spring and improvement and John Anderson's Spring & improvement; Uriah Anderson locator.

211. Nov. 1, 1803 Edward Gwin, assignee of Robert Pearce of Sion Perry of James Moss sole heir of John Middleton heir of Robert Moss; warrant 4131; 640 ac in Jackson Co, on N side of "Comberland" [R], begins on the river bank 10 poles above mouth of Dry Cr, runs up the river, North, & includes John Black improvement & plantation; John Black locator; reentered Sept. 16, 1807 "W C".

p. 98
212. Nov. 1, 1803 Isaac Taylor, assignee of Winey Norton; due to "sertericate"

from military warrant 41 for 640 ac assignee of Winey Norton "hairs" of William Norten private; 502.5 ac on N side of Spring Cr of Roaring R, on waters of same, begins "a small" distance E of corner of 1,000 ac granted to John Rice on a "pereral" due N 200 poles from Rice's line, runs E, S for complement, bounded by survey of Christian "Rodes" on E, "the same" on S & Rice's line; Isaac Taylor locator.

213. Nov. 4, 1803 Garret Fitzgerald, assignee of Charles J Love of Porter of "Jobesmith" John Somuner; warrant 4338; 640 ac on N side of Cumbereland R, begins on left hand fork of first creek that puts in Cumberland [R] below old Mr. Sanders, begins NW 30 poles of Scantling's Camps, "rund" S, E, & "sorrund" for complement; John "Tuhaye" locator; this entry made void by order of Garret Futzgerald Dec. 31.

p. 99
214. Nov. 7, 1803 Garret Fitzgerald, assignee of William Misether(maybe), warrant 1482 from Carter's office; 50 ac, begins on Hennary McKenney line so as to run up Trap Br on both sides for quantity; Garret Fitzgerald locator; Nov. 7, 1807 I transfer this entry to Jonathan Noble (signed) Garret Fitzgerald; set void by order of Jonathan Noble "18th"; Jul. 13 [or 18], 1804 (written sideways on right side).

215. Nov. 7, 1803 Garret Fitzgerreld, assignee of J Coman of Stokley Donelson of Walter Jinsey; due to military warrant 4495 assignee of J Coman of "Stokley" Donelson of Walter Linsey; 74 ac, begins at fork of Harrican Ridge, runs down both sides of "the creek", includes Isums Spring and improvement where Oldnel [or Olddell] lived; Garret Fitzgerald locator.

p. 100
216. Nov. 8, 1803 David Spears; warrant 3730; 799 ac in Jackson Co on N side of Cumberland R, on waters of Barron [R], begins about 0.5 miles below John Fowler & "Suliienus" Fowlere, runs as law directs, includes said Fowlers' improvement where they live for complement; A Stubblefield locator.

217. Nov. 8, 1803 John Deal assignee of "Fanses" Maybury; warrant 350; 100 ac begins at mouth of my spring branch, runs "tdo" branch 120 [poles], N, W to the river, with the river to beginning for quantity; John "Dale" locator.

p. 101
217A [no number]. (no date) Lawson "Nrerse", assignee of Howel Tatum; warrant "rong woost"; 100 ac due to warrant 114 signed by William "Mclin" in Jackson Co on "southerly" fork of Sugar Cr, includes the "fo".

218. Dec. 26, 1803 Carter "Gellon", assignee of Moses Fisk; warrant 324; 100 ac, due to William Maclin warrant 324, in Jackson Co on waters of Roaring R,

westerly of "Mr Offiser's", includes improvement & house where said Dillon lives; Moses Fisk locator.

219. Dec. 26, 1803 Lawson Nreres, assignee of Howel Tatum; due to William Maclin warrant 114; 100 ac in Jackson Co, on southerly fork of Sugar Cr, includes the falls usually called the mill seat or mill "shooles" (sic) and tree marked "4 H" that stands "just" above said falls; made void by order of Lawson Nreres [or Nures], made void by me Isaac Fisk.

p. 102.
220. Jan. 2, 1804 [location of land of seventy three ac--lined out] [no name]; warrant 5220; 73 ac ac on waters of Roaring R, begins at chesnut marked "C" and a "dimond" below the "C", runs S & N for complement, includes improvement made by "the" Williams; "Binjamin" Blackburn locator.

221. Aug. 9, 1804 Isaac Fisk, assignee of James Maxwell; due to military warrant 4225 issued by James Glasgow to William Dixon and sold by his heir Jerimiah Dixon to James Maxwell, and Isaac Fisk is assignee of said Maxwell [additional sales mentioned in Tennessee Revolutionary War warrants roll 7]; 640 ac in Jackson Co in first large bottom above Little Island Cr, about 10 or 2 miles above Roaring R, begins near mouth of small branch that runs into Cumberland R "nigh" lower end of said bottom, runs up the river, & off for complement; Isaac Fisk locator.

p. 103.
222. Aug. 9, 1804 Hugh Kuester [or Krester]; military warrant 765 issued by James Glasgow; 274 ac in Jackson Co on S side of Cumberland R, in first bottom above mouth of Little Island Cr, begins on "nor" bank at upper corner of Isaac Fisk's 640 ac entry, runs with said tract, & up the river for complement; "Isaack" Fisk locator; [warrant 765 issued to Hugh "Hueston" who served in fourth and first regiments, and see Revolutionary War Pension file W8929 by wife Martha Huston].

223. (no date) James Davis, assignee of Andrew Basselman; "military" warrant 291 signed by William Maclin; 320 ac in Jackson Co on S side of Cumberland R, begins at a small banch "nigh" upper end of first bottom above mouth of Little Cr, runs down the river & "off" for complement; Isaac Fisk locator.

p. 104
224. Aug. 9, 1804 Isaac Fisk, assignee of Samuel Jackson; "military" warrant 234 signed by William Maclin; 100 ac in Jackson Co in first bottom on S side of Cumberland R below Hameltons Ferry, begins "ner" upper end of said bottom, runs down the river, & "off" for complement; includes a "caben" & improvement near Henderson's Ferry; Isaac Fisk locator.

225. Aug. 9, 1804 Isaac Fisk, assignee of Samuel Jackson; "military" warrant 243 signed by William Maclin; 50 ac on S side of Cumberland R, begins on a West fork of big Island Cr at 2 beach trees about 0.5 miles from the "pention", about 1.5 miles from said river, runs E, W, & N for complement; Isaac Fisk locator.

p. 105
226. Aug. 9, 1804 "Ferdenand" Hamilton, assignee of Samuel Fish; "military" warrant 233 signed by William Maclin; 100 ac in Jackson Co on "a" Mill Cr, begins at large beech marked "E H" on S side of said beech, runs S, W for complement, & includes "improve" where James Laxton lives.

227. Aug. 9, 1804 Moses Fisk, assignee of Sampson Williams, assignee of Stokley Donelson & William Terrrell assignees of [William Keith] heir of John Keith; military warrant 3636; 640 ac in Jackson Co on high lands between Roaring R & Sampsons Fork of Mill Cr, begins at chesnut & poplar corner of William "Turrell" Lewis' location of warrant 5193, runs W, & N for quantity; Moses Tusk [or Fisk] locator.

p. 106
228. Aug. 9, 1804 Moses Fisk; warrant 329 signed by William Maclin; 50 ac on Copers Cr, includes "the cascades" or mill seat on said creek near Carter Dilson's, runs to best advantage for quantity; Moses Fisk locator.

229. (no date) Isaac Fisk, assignee of Howel Tatum; "military" warrant 94 signed by William Maclin; 88.5 ac in Jackson Co on Sugar Cr, begins at sugar tree on E bank of the creek, runs S, E for complement, includes cabin and small improvement where Mr. Abner [or Alener] lives; Isaac Fisk locator.

p. 107
230. Aug. 9, 1804 Howel Tatum, assignee of Dannel [or Darnel] Lettory; "military" warrant 509 signed by William Maclin; 86.75 ac in Jackson Co on N fork of Mill Cr, formerly called Lick Cr, begins at a beach & hickory marked [sort of square "B"] nigh where said creek forks, runs S, & E for complement; "Lowson" Nurs locator.

231. Aug. 9, 1804 Isaac Fisk, assignee of Howel Tatum; "military" warrant 117 signed by William Maclin; 100 ac in Jackson Co on Sugar Cr about 2 miles from its mouth, begins at an elm on E bank of said creek, runs S, & W for complement; Isaac Fisk, locator.

p. 108
232. Aug. 9, 1804 Isaac Fisk, assignee of Moses Fisk; warrant 328 signed by William Maclin; 50 ac in Jackson Co, begins at [white--lined out] NW corner of Charles Dillon's land at white oak marked "I O", runs S, & W for complement; Lawson Nourses locator.

233. Aug. 9, 1804 Moses Fisk, assignee of Peter Persey "heirs" of John Persey; military warrant 2869; 60 ac in Jackson Co on S side of Cumberland R, joins said river, above grant to George "Cumninrs", includes mouth of large branch of brook that runs into Cumberland [R] between said grant to "Cummiars" & Colemon's [or Colemors] preemption at mouth of "Oby" [R].

p. 109
234. Aug. 9, 1804 Lawson Nourse, assignee of Howel Tatum; "military" warrant 114 signed by William Maclin; 100 ac in Jackson Co on Sampsons Fork, a branch of Mill Cr, begins at point of a ridge at white oak & sugar tree marked "L N", runs N, W for complement, includes plantation where Mr. Skeggs lives; Lawson Nourse locator.

235. Jul. 15, 1805 Moses Fisk, assignee of Thomas Dillon, T Scurlock [or Sceerlock] & J Dawes; military warrant 5160; 640 ac in Jackson Co on N side of Cumberland R, begins at mouth of Dry Cr, runs N, up said river for complement, includes a large branch or brook on mouth thereof known as Black's Br; Moses Fisk locator.

p. 110
236. Sept. 6, 1805 Andrew Peddy, assignee of Spencer Griffin assignee of Joel Pendor heir of Benjamin Pendor; military warrant 2871; 640 ac in Jackson Co on S side of Cumberland R, in a bend above Little Island Cr, "to be" above heirs of William Rhoades' 1,000 ac that begins opposite mouth of Brimstone Cr, begins on river bank at upper corner of said 1,000 acres, runs up the river, "off" for quantity, on E side of said "Rhodes"; located by Moses Fisk, for one undivided moiety of same; [see Tennessee Revolutionary War warrants roll 4 for warrant & sales of same].

237. Sept. 6, 1804 heirs of William Rhodes; military warrant 3285; 1,000 ac in Jackson Co on S side of Cumberland R, in a bend above Little Island Cr, begins on river bank opposite mouth of Brimstone Cr, runs up & down the river, "off" for quantity; located by Moses Fisk for one undivided moiety of same; [see Tennessee Revolutionary War warrants roll 5 for many sales of parts of the warrant].

(238). [on last page of book, not numbered] Oct. 24, 1806 I transfer 160 ac to John Hancock being part of 640 ac survey that James Bedford & Edmond Roberts bought and part of this tansfer lays in Bedford's & "Robert", the location stands in p. 14 location 42 date of entry Jul. 5, 1802, it is understood if land is lost I am not bound to make it good, said Hancock has no recourse from me (signed) Christopher Bullard [Bullar, on location 42] (witness) J Muford.

(239). [on loose sheet] "Oct. 24" I transfer 160 ac to James Bedford, being part of

640 ac survey "made John Fitzgerald entry boock", being part of entry that Edmond Roberts bought, part of said transfer join s "Parkr's" line, location is No. 42 on p. 14 dated Jul. 5, 1802, if land is lots, I am not bound to "mak" it good, said Bedford has no "recorse" back on me (signed) Christopher Bullard (witness) J Muford.

series 2 book 55 [Davidson Co] entry book 1802-1803

[locations 1-6 missing; no page numbers in book, about 2 locations (sometimes 3) per page]

240 (7). Feb. 26, 1802 Alexander McMillen & Thomas Shannon; [military] warrant 3793; 640 ac on waters of S Harpeth, supposed to be in Davidson Co, near southern boundary line thereof, same not being yet assertained between "and" Williamson County, begins on W bank of said Harpeth [R} or near there, "to" about 60 poles above mouth of Hunting Camp Cr, N, & E to include 640 ac; Thomas Shannon locator.

no 8, skip in numbers

241 (9). Apr. 13, 1802 John Buchanan, assignee of Richard Cooke assignee of Abraham Thrift heir of Miles Thrift; [military] warrant 4787; 640 ac on waters of Mill Cr, joins Saml Buchanan's original guard "rite" and Edward Cox, also South boundary line of survey where Jeremiah Grizzard lives; John Buchanan locator; "Jan. 20" record my warrant 4787 for 640 ac (signed) John Buchanan.

242 (10). Apr. 14, 1802 heirs of William White; warrant 4791; 640 ac on S side of Cumberland R, on big Harpeth R, begins on William Gillaspie's line at an ash on river bank, runs E 200 poles with said line to stake on Thomas Edmondson's line, S 160 poles with said line to white oak & sugar tree, E 337 poles to stake, S 350 poles to stake, W 147 poles to William Stewart's SE corner poplar & elm, N 290 poles with Stewart's line to his NE corner beech & hickory, 145 poles down meanders of the river to Stewart's beginning 2 black oaks, W 220 poles with said Stewart's line to box elder & ash on bank of W Hapeth [R], down meanders of the river to beginning; above location supposed to be in Davidson Co; Richd Cooke locator; recd. Dec. 6, 1802 my warrant 4791 (signed) Richd Cooke.

243 (11). Apr. 19, 1802 Edward Harris, assignee of Charles Smallwood assignee of Polly Richards of Burke; [military] warrant 3274; 640 ac on S side of E fork of Stone R, joins 640 ac granted to Robert Weakley on S, 1,508 ac tract in John Welch's name on West, runs S, & W for complement; (no locator); Jul. 5, 1803 removed by R Weakley.

244 (12). Apr. 19, 1802 Edward Harris, assignee of Henry Bonner heir of John & James Bonner assignee of Isaac Denis; warrant 2997; 274 ac on S side of E fork of Stones R, joins 640 ac granted to Griffith Rutherford on S, runs S, & W for complement; (no locator); recd. above warrant 2997 for 274 ac Apr. 14, 1807 (signed) R Weakley.

245 (13). Apr. 30, 1802 John Buchanan, assignee of Richard Cooke assignee of Abraham Thrift heir of Miles Thrift; warrant 4737; 575 ac on Mill Cr waters, joins N & E boundary lines of 640 ac grant to said John Buchanan assignee of William Mobley, joins S boundary of survey granted to Sutherlin Mayfield "next" below Thomas Lightfoot; John Buchanan locator; Jan. 20, 1807 recd. my warrant 4737 for 575 ac (signed) John Buchanan.

246 (14). May 12, 1802 James Marshal, assignee of George B Curtis assignee of Stokely Donnelson assignee of Robert Flinn; warrant 4303; 640 ac in Davidson Co on S side of Whites Cr, begins near head of "wright" hand fork of Larkings Br, being S of said Marshal house, runs N, & W for complement; (no locator); recd warrant May 19, 1807 (signed) James "Marshall".

247 (15). Jun. 7, 1802 John White, assignee of James Davis assignee of Robert Nelson assignee of Alexander Nelson assignee of John Law heir of Richard Law; warrant 3773; 274 ac on waters of Stones R, joins W boundary line of 400 ac grant to Samuel Buchanan, on part of which tract Simon McLendan lives, begins 30 poles N of "whare" said line crosses Cave Spring Br, runs W, & S; John White locator; recd. this warrant May 12, 1807 (signed) John White.

248 (16). Jun. 11, 1802 Robert Weakley; warrant 8; 164 ac in Davidson Co on W side of Stewarts Cr, begins on William L Alexander's S boundary line at Robert Weakley's corner of 274 ac tract, runs S with line of said tract to Edward Cox's N boundary line, W with said complement; R Weakley locator; recd. above warrant No. 8 for 164 ac Apr. 14, 1807 (signed) R Weakley.

249 (17). Jun. 11, 1802 Robert Weakley; warrant 9; 187 ac on W side of Stones R, between mouh of E fork of said river & Stewarts Cr, includes large spring near the river, begins at 2 small red oaks on W bank of said river below said spring on Robert Smith's line, runs W with said line to Stephen Cantrell's line, S with said Cantrell's line to said Weakley's corner of another tract, E with line of said tract to "the" corner, S to Joseph Martin's line, E with Martin's line & passing his corner to the river, down meanders of the river to beginning; R Weakley locator; recd. above warrant No. 9 for 187 ac Apr. 14, 1807 R Weakley.

250 (18). Jun. 11, 1802 Robert Weakley; warrant 11; 89 ac on N side of Cumberland R, on W fork of Heatons Cr, joins land of John Drake on W, runs W up both sides of said fork, includes place where James Hatfield lives; R Weakley locator; May 27, 1803 I assign my right of this location to James Hatfield (signed) R Weakley; recd. above warrant No. 11 Apr. 14, 1807 (signed) R Weakley.

251 (19). Jun. 11, 1802 Robert Weakley; warrant 14; 69 ac on N side of Cumberland R, on both sides of Sulpher Cr, begins at Thomas Pierce's NE corner white ash on E side of the creek, runs W 37 chains with his line to his corner, N

9.75 chains to stake, E to Reaves corner, with his line same course in all 37 chains, & S to beginning; R Weakley locator; recd. above warrant No. 14 for 69 ac Apr. 14, 1807 (signed) R Weakley.

252 (20). Jun. 11, 1802 James Russell, assignee of Robert Weakley; warrant 10; 200 ac on S side of Cumberland R, on both sides of "Sames" Cr, begins at NE corner of James Russell's 274 ac tract poplar & beach marked "RW" on E bank of the creek, runs N, & E for complement; James Russell locator; recd. above warrant No. 10 for 200 ac Apr. 14, 1807 (signed) R Weakley.

253 (21). Jun. 11, 1802 James Marshal, assignee of George B Curtis assignee of Stokeley Donelson assignee of Robert Flinn; [military] warrant 4308; 525 ac due to certificate originating from above warrant, on waters of Whites Cr, begins about 40 poles above Matthias "Prock's" improvement where he lives, on W side of said Prock's Br, runs S, & E for complement; James Marshal locator.

254 (22). Jun. 16, 1802 James Hamilton, assignee of Robert Nelson assignee of Joseph Hopkins; warrant (blank, maybe Evans Battalion); 400 ac in Davidson Co on waters of Stones R, on Hamiltons Cr, runs up & down the creek for complement, includes improvement where said Hamilton lives; James Hamilton locator; recd. above warrant No (blank) for 400 ac Apr. 21, 1807 (signed) Jas Hamilton (witness) John C McLemore.

255 (23). Jun. 26, 1802 Thomas Shute, assignee of Thomas Dillon attorney for Joseph Scurlock assignee of Robert Barge; [military] warrant 3993; 640 ac in Davidson Co on waters of Stuarts Cr, begins at Cox's NW corner, runs N to Alexander's S boundary line, W with his line, & S for complement; Thomas Shute locator; recd. warrant 3993 for 640 ac Apr. 10, 1807 (signed) Thomas Shute (witness) John C McLemore.
        no 24, skip in numbers

256 (25). Aug. 26, 1802 Enoch Douge, assignee of Caleb Berry; [military] warrant 3992; 274 ac in Davidson Co on S side of Cumberland R, on "Salms" Cr, joins James Russell's 274 ac entry above, runs up the creek as law directs, includes the vacant land; James Russell locator.

257 (26). Aug. 26, 1802 Samuel Ferebee, assignee of Dempsey Cassey of Jesse Cox; [military] warrant 5010; 274 ac in Davidson Co on S side of Cumberland R, near dividing ridge between Harpeth [R] & Cumberland [R], on head waters of Bluff Cr, begins at poplar tree marked as corner, runs W, S as law directs, includes a spring & tree marked "J R"; James Russell locator.

258 (27). Aug. 28, 1802 Jacob Holt, assignee of Stockly Donelson assignee of Charles Thomas originally; [military] warrant 4295; 428 ac in Davidson Co, on both sides of fork of Whites Cr that crosses the road from Stump's to Clarkesville,

includes said Holt's improvement, joins survey made by Robert Hays; Will Lytle jr; Nov. 9, 1802 this location removed by me (signed) Will Lytle.

259 (28). Sept. 25, 1802 John & Ephraim C Davidson, assignee of James Espey; warrant (blank); 640 ac on E fork of Stones R, on SW side of said (blank) Fork, begins 400 poles S of Hancock's SW corner originally surveyed for Robert Weakly on side of knob, joins John & Ephraim C Davidson's 1,000 ac entry on S, runs as law directs, includes the vacant land; John & Ephraim C Davidson locators; (no date) removed Ephraim Davidson "locator".

260 (29). Sept. 27, 1802 John & Ephraim C Davidson, assignees of Wily "Chery" assignee of William Brazell; [military] warrant 43; 1,000 ac on E fork of Stones R on SW side, begins on S boundary line of Edward Harris' 640 ac entry of tract originally surveyed for Griffith Rutherford, runs as law directs, includes the vacant land; John & Ephraim C Davidson locator.

261 (30). Oct. 27, 1802 Howel Tatum, assignee of Robert Searcy assignee of James McCafferty assignee of Thomas Smith assignee of John Upton; [military] warrant 2439; 640 ac in Davidson Co on waters of Manskers Cr & Dry Cr, joins lines of Mansker's Lick survey, Peter Cloud's survey, others, & extends westwardly for complement; Ho Tatum locator; removed Jun. 7, 1803 (signed) Ho Tatum.

262 (31). Oct. 27, 1802 Howel Tatum, assignee of James L White assignee of Stockley Donelson attorney for Robert Huff; [military] warrant 4090; 640 ac in Davidson Co on waters of Dry Cr, joins W boundary of the pubic survey that includes Mansker's Lick, and lines of other surveys for quantity; Howel Tatum locator; removed by Ho Tatum Jun. 13, 1803.

263 (32). Nov. 12, 1802 Thomas Shute, assignee of Philip Shute; warrant 71; 100 ac in Davidson Co on waters of Hurricane [Cr], begins on N boundary of Stockly "Dolleson's" tract that joins Ebenezar Brooks on NE corner, runs N, & W for complement; Thomas Shute locator; recd. above warrant No 71 for 100 ac Apr. 10, 1807 (signed) Thomas Shute (witness) J C McLemore; reentered Jul. 28, 1809 (not signed).

264 (33). Nov. 12, 1802 Thomas Shute, assignee of Philip Shute; warrant 72; 50 ac in Davidson Co on waters of E fork of Mill Cr, begins on E boundary of said Thomas Shute's tract that joins Lardner Clark on SW corner, runs E, S for complement; Thomas Shute locator; recd. above warrant No. 72 for 50 ac Apr. 10, 1807 (signed) Thomas Shute (witness) John C McLemore; reentered Jul. 28, 1809 (not signed).

265 (34). Nov. 12, 1802 Thomas Shute, assignee of Philip Shute; warrant 69; 100 ac in Davidson Co on waters of Hurricane [Cr], begins at hickory tree about "one

mild" westwardly from mouth of Hurricane [Cr], West of a large glade, near a path to mouth of Hurricane [Cr], runs E, & S for quantity; Thomas Shute locator; recd. above warrant No 69 for 100 ac Apr. 10, 1807 (signed) Thomas Shute (witness) J C McLemore; reentered Jul. 29, 1809 (not signed).

266 (35). Nov. 12, 1802 Thomas Shute, assignee of Philip Shute; warrant 70; 100 ac in Davidson Co on waters of Stewarts Cr, begins on W boundary of said Thomas Shute's tract that joins Edward Cox on West, runs W, & S for complement; Thomas Shute locator; recd. above warrant No 70 for 100 ac Apr. 10, 1807 (signed) Thomas Shute (witness) J C McLemore; reentered Jul. 28, 1809 (not signed).

267 (36). Nov. 12, 1802 Thomas Shute, assignee of Philip Shute; warrant 74; 88 ac in Davidson Co on waters of Hurricane [Cr], begins on N boundary of land formerly belonging to McGoodon, Hartwell Seats lives on part of of said tract, runs N, & W for complement; Thomas Shute locator; recd. above warrant No 74 for 88 ac Apr. 10, 1807 (signed) Thomas Shute & J C McLemore; reentered Jul. 28, 1809 (not signed).

268 (37). Nov. 12, 1802 Thomas Shute, assignee of Philip Shute; warrant 73; 50 ac in Davidson Co on waters of Hurricane Cr, begins at a hickory tree, runs N, E for quantity, includes a sink hole spring lying N of Ebenezar Brooks, W of Stockly Donnelson, "which land" has been entered in their names; Thomas Shute locator; Jul. 14, 1803 this entry removed by me (signed) Thomas Shute.
     no 38, skip in numbers

269 (39). Nov. 12, 1802 John G Blount, assignee of Hardy Whitly, William Whitly, & Arther Whitly, heirs of William Whitly deceased; [military] warrant 3987; 640 ac on eastern branches of W fork of Stones R, joins Sarah Rutledge's land on E, runs along "hur" line, & eastwardly for complement; Apr. 8, 1807 recd warrant No 3989 for 640 ac (signed) John Donelson (witness) J C McLemore.0

270 (40). Dec. 2, 1802 William Galbraith, assignee of George Smith sr; warrant 668; 428 ac in Davidson Co, joins Col. Robert Hays' land on Suges Cr, includes 2 springs of said creek & 2 small improvements I bought of Thomas Smothers, runs for complement; (no locator); Aug. 18, 1803 this entry removed by me (signed) John Galbraith, agent of Wm Galbraith.

271 (41). Dec. 10, 1802 Edward "Herris", assignee of Henry Broner assignee of George Cook; [military] warrant 2995; 1,000 ac on waters of E fork of Stones R, joins said Herris' 640 ac entry on West, joins John & Ephraim C Davidson's entry on North, runs as law directs to include the vacant land; Ephraim C Davidson locator.

272 (42). Jan. 4, 1803 William Galispie & David Dobbins, assignee of George

Smith assignee of Redmond D Barry assignee of Norris Bowsman; warrant 5239; 640 ac in Davidson Co on McCutchins Spring Br, joins James Dickson on East, John Curren & John Rains on South, Thomas Lightfoot on West "if possible", & runs courses agreeable to law for complement; David Dobbins locator; Sept. 19, 1803 this entry removed by me today (signed) David Dobbins.

273 (43). Jan. 8, 1803 Abraham Sett [or Scott], assignee of Evin Pannell; warrant 5285; 274 ac on E fork of Stones R, begins on Gideon Rucker's N boundary line, runs N, & E for complement; (no locator).

274 (44). Jan. 15, 1803 John Motharal, assignee of Samuel Shannon; warrant 87; 100 ac on waters of Whites Cr, begins at beech marked "I M" & sugar tree "a few" poles E of said Motharal's barn, runs W, S for complement, includes said Motharal's house & improvement; S Shannon locator; reentered May 12, 1809 (not signed).

275 (45). Jan. 15, 1803 Samuel Shannon; warrant 86; 50 ac in Davidson Co on waters of Manskers Cr, includes place where Thomas "Dicxson" formerly lived, part of improvement Jesse Walker made, begins on N boundary of land Robert Ewing "laid", runs N, & E for complement; S Shannon locator.

276 (46). Jan. 15, 1803 Samuel Shannon; warrant 85; 50 ac in Davidson Co on waters of Whites Cr, begins on Alexander Reed's S boundary, runs S, W for complement, includes place where Peter Johnson formerly made sugar; S Shannon locator; (no date) today I transferred my right & interest in this entry to James Johnson for value received (signed) S Shannon.

277 (47). Jan. 15, 1803 Samuel Shannon; warrant 84; 10 ac on Clay Lick Fork of Whites Cr, includes falls of said creek that is above Dunkin's claim, begins on W side of said creek, runs E, & N for complement; S Shannon locator; reentered Nov. 24, 1809 (not signed).

278 (48). Jan. 18, 1803 Robert Weakley; warrant 97; 161 ac on both sides of E fork of Stones R, begins on N side of said fork on eastern boundary line of said Robert Weakley & Thomas Bedford's 3,840 ac [shuck 2468A in Davidson Co in NC grants], runs E, S, & as law directs for complement; R Weakley locator; recd. warrant 97 for 161 on Apr. 14, 1807 (signed) R Weakley.

279 (49). Jan. 24, 1803 John & Ephraim C Davidson, assignee of James Espie; warrant (blank); 640 ac on waters of Lytles Cr, about 2 miles in West direction from Capt. Binges' "living" on waters of Cripple Cr, begins 40 poles NE of a spring rising among some ceders with several deer paths leading to it, runs as law directs, & includes the vacant land; John & Ephraim C Davidson locators.

280 (50). Jan. 27, 1803 Jacob Holt, assignee of George Garrett assignee of Stockly

Donelson assignee of Charles Thomas; [military] warrant 4295; 148 ac on head waters of Whites Cr, on both sides of "mane" road from Nashville to Clarksville, begins at large poplar & beech on W side of the creek, runs E 40 chains to white oak & beech, S 37 chains to large sugar tree on Col. Robert Hays' N boundary of 640 ac tract, & as law directs for complement; William Lytle locator; reentered Jun. 16, 1809 (not signed).

no 51 through 63, skip in numbers 281 (64). May 12, 1803 Robert Weakley, assignee of George B Curtis; warrant 104; 100 ac on Lockes Cr, North waters of E fork of Stones R, joins Matthew Lock's 428 ac grant on upper side, runs up both sides of said creek, includes vacant land for complement; R Weakley locator; recd. warrant 104 for 100 ac Apr. 14, 1807 (signed) R Weakley.

282 (65). May 23, 1803 James Donelley; warrant 259; 53 ac in Davidson Co on waters of Richland Cr, begins at a beech marked "D" on said Donelley's S boundary of tract where he lives, runs W, & S for complement; James "Donlley" locator; recd. warrant 259 for 53 ac May 22, 1807 (signed) John Donelly's mark "X".

283 (66). May 23, 1803 May 23, 1803 Daniel Wheaton; warrant 23; 12 ac, begins at most southerly corner of lot 165 "joining" Nashville, runs S "some degrees" West with the academy line to "the" corner, N "some degrees W" with "accademy" line to McNair's line, N "some degrees" East to back line of the down, & with town line to beginning Daniel Weaton locator.

284 (67). May 27, 1803 Isaac Shute, assignee of Thomas Shute; warrant 926; 150 ac in Davidson Co, on waters of Hurricane Cr, due to certificate originated from warrant 926, begins on W boundary of Thomas Shute's entry as assignee of Robert Weakley, runs W, N, & includes a sink hole spring; Isaac Shute locator; Dec. 27, 1806 recd. warrant 926 of this location (signed) Isaac Shute.

285 (68). Jun. 2, 1803 Thomas Shute & Beel Bosley, joint assignees of Thomas "Dillin" assignee of Richard Russell heir of Andrew Russell; [military] warrant 2876; 640 ac in Davidson Co on waters of E fork of W fork of Stones R "or" Lytles Cr, begins on S boundary of "Pearcen's" grant of which part is owned by William & Joseph Gowen & now lives on, runs W, S for complement, includes house & plantation where James Garner lives; Thomas Shute locator; recd. warrant 2876 for 640 ac Apr. 10, 1807 (signed) Thomas Shute (witness) John C McLemore.

286 (69). Jun. 7, 1803 Charles Boiles, assignee of Daniel Wheaton; warrant 269; 35 ac in Davidson Co on N side of Cumberland R, on waters of Whites Cr, joins James Marshall's line, begins 15 poles S of where his upper line crosses the creek, includes vacant land between said Marshall and "Cloyd" for complement; Charles Boiles locator; removed by me Jul. 27, 1802 (signed) C Boiles.

287 (70). Jun. 11, 1803 Ebenezer Rice, assignee of Samuel Shannon; warrant 93 50 ac in Davidson Co near Indian Cr, begins at beech tree marked "D R" within 17 rods of said creek which is original corner of land I purchased of Charles Hutton, on line now occupied by William Killum, runs W 88 rods, N 92 rods, E 88 [rods], S 92 rods to first mentioned beginning as law directs, includes "the" vacant land; Ebenezer Rice locator.

288 (71). Jun. 13, 1803 Howel Tatum, assignee of James L White assignee of Stockly Donelson attorney for Robert Huff; [military] warrant 4090; 640 ac on waters of E fork of Stones R, joins S boundary of land of heirs of Henry Wiggins deceased, runs South up both sides of a creek for complement; [Nov. 28, 1806 today I removed this entry & recd my warrant--lined out & not signed]; Dec. 22, 1806 recd. my warrant (signed) Ho Tatum.

289 (72). Jun. 15, 1803 James Marshall, assignee of Daniel Wheaton; warrant 286; 40 ac on N side of Cumberland R, on waters of Whites Cr, begins on West boundary line of B Boiles, runs West for complement, includes spring known as Otter Spring; Charles Boiles locator; reentered Jul. 30, 1808 (not signed).

290 (73). Jun. 15, 1803 Charles Boiles, assignee of Daniel Wheaton; warrant 267; 35 ac on N side of Cumberland R, on waters of Whites Cr, joins George Taylor on West, runs up & down "the" branch for complement; Charles Boiles locator.

291 (74). Jan. 15, 1803 Charles Boiles, assignee of Daniel Wheaton; warrant 270; 40 ac on N side of Cumberland R, on waters of Whites [Cr], joins his other entry on warrant 267 on upper line, runs up "the" branch for complement; Charles Boiles.

292 (75). Jun. 18, 1803 Joseph Hooper & Charles Boiles, equal owners, assignees of Samuel Shannon; warrant 92; 50 ac on N side of Cumberland R, on waters of Whites Cr, includes house & plantation where William McKnight formerly lived and whereon "one" Morris now lives for complement; Charles Boiles locator.

293 (76). Jun. 18, 1803 Joseph Hooper & Charles Boiles, equal owners, assignees of Samuel Shannon; warrant 88; 30 ac in Davidson Co on N side of Cumberland R, begins & runs to include house & improvement where "one" Isaac Williams lives for complement, house & "plantation" to be near the center; Charles Boiles locator.

294 (77). Jun. 29, 1803 William Orman, assignee of Daniel Wheaton; warrant 287; 50 ac on Locks Cr, North waters of East fork of Stones R, joins Robert Weakley's entry on upper side, runs up both sides of said creek, includes a small improvement & a spring "rising in" the creek; William Orman locator; (no date) wntry made void & warrant "lifted" by William Orman's order.

295 (78). Jun. 30, 1803 Stewart Fambrough, assignee of Robert Weakley; due to certificate from warrant 14; 33 ac in Davidson Co on N side of Cumberland R, on waters of Sulpher Cr, includes cabbin & improvement made by David Hood, runs to include the good land joining said cabbin; Stewart Fambrough locator.

296 (79). Jul. 12, 1803 "Endmond Dihons"; warrant 6; 1,000 ac in Davidson Co on E fork of Stones R, begins at Reed's SE corner of 640 ac tract where Alexander Moore lives, runs E, & N for complement; Thomas Mitchell locator; Jan. 1, 1807 recd. Edmond Dukons' warrant No. 6 for 1,000 ac (signed) Tho McCpel [or McLepel].

297 (80). Jul. 13, 1803 Robert Hewitt & Thomas Shute, joint assignees of Thomas Dillin assignee of John Stone heir of Zedekiah Stone; [military] warrant 2883; 640 ac in Davidson Co on Stewart [Cr], a branch of Stones R, "in" about 2 or 3 miles of said creek above Harts Spring, includes a large sink hole spring with some trees killed about it and tree marked "T S ꓕ M", "those marks" made "several" years ago it is said by Thomas Spencer & John Mulherin, runs as law directs to include the best vacant land; Thomas Shute locator; Apr. 10, 1807 recd. above warrant 2883 for 640 ac (signed) Thomas Shute (witness) John C McLemore.

298 (81). Jul. 14, 1803 Thomas Shute, assignee of Philip Shute; warrant 73; 50 ac in Davidson Co on Mill Cr, begins on James McQuistin's SW corner on side of his mill "ponn", runs W across said mill ponn to John Buchanan's SE corner, N with said Buchanan's line for complement; Apr. 10, 1807 recd. above warrant 73 for 50 ac (signed) Thomas Shute (witness) J C McLemore; reentered Jul. 28, 1809 (not signed).

299 (82). Jul. 26, 1803 Isaac Coffman, assignee of Daniel Wheaton; warrant 281; 50 ac in Davidson Co on waters of Whites Cr, begins at sugar tree on Jacob Stump's line, runs N, & E to include "the" vacant land; Isaac Coffman locator.

300 (83). Jul. 29, 1803 Francis "Youraa", assignee of David Earheart; warrant 98; 200 ac in Davidson Co on waters of Cripple Cr, begins at a black oak & ash, runs S to "the" Indian line, & W for complement; Francis Youraa locator; Mar. 18, 1807 recd. my warrant 98 for 200 ac "of" this entry (signed) Francis "Youree" (witness) J C McLemore.

301 (84). Jul. 29, 1803 Francis Youraa, assignee of David Earheart; warrant 99; 184 ac in Davidson Co, on waters of Cripple Cr, begins 50 poles from NE corner of Francis Youraa's line on W side of his 200 ac tract, runs S, & W for complement; Francis Youraa locator; Jul. 1, 1806 today I removed this entry & received my warrant (signed) "Frances" Youree.

302 (85). Jul. 30, 1803 John Lucas, assignee of James Marshall assignee of G B

Curtis; [military] warrant 4308; 209 ac on N side of Cumberland R, on waters of Whites Cr, begins at Stump's E boundary line at small beech tree marked "⅃ L", runs E, N for complement, includes my house & plantation; John Lucas locator.

303 (86). Aug. 8, 1803 Thomas Armstrong, assignee of Patrick Ryan sergeant; warrant 301; 1,000 ac in Davidson Co on Cripple Cr, a branch of E fork of Stones R, joins "Readon" Blount's 640 ac tract on E boundary, runs as law directs to include said 1,000 ac; Wm Nash locator; Feb. 19, 1807 recd. warrant 301 of this location for 1,000 ac (signed) Wm Nash.

304 (87). Aug. 12, 1803 Thomas Shute & Robert Hewitt, assignees of Thomas Dillin assignee of John Sebaston heir of Stephen Sebaston; [military] warrant 3021; 640 ac in Davidson Co on waters of Stewarts Cr, joins Hardiman on South boundary line, Bowen on North & W boundary lines, runs as law directs to include the best vacant land; Thomas Shute locator; Apr. 10, 1807 recd. above warrant 3021 for 640 ac (signed) Thomas Shute (witness) J C McLemore.

305 (88). Aug. 23, 1803 Daniel Joslin, assignee of William Lytle jr who is heir of Andrew Lytle deceased; warrant 5112; 360 ac on Turnbulls Cr, includes John Simmons improvement where said Simmons lives, begins on Thompson's line, runs up the creek, & as law directs for complement; Daniel Joslin locator; Sept. 10, 1806 I assign my right of this entry to William Lytle jr for value received (signed) Daniel Joslin's mark "X" (witness) Tho Childress; (no date) recd. my warrant 5112 for 360 ac "by" Danl Joslin to me (signed) Wm Lytle jr.

306 (89). Aug. 24, 1803 Daniel "Southalan", assignee of Frederick Harper; warrant 1509; 640 ac on head waters of W fork of Stones R, joins William Nash's 428 ac survey on part of West boundary, begins at NW corner honey locust, runs S, & W for quantity; F Harper locator; May 1, 1807 recd. this warrant (signed) J M Lewis.

307 (90). Aug. 31, 1803 Hugh Robison, assignee of Howel Tatum; warrant 261; 100 ac on waters of Overalls Fork, begins on South boundary line of Howel Tatum's 228 ac entry, runs S with Armstrong's line, W with "said Tatom's" line for complement; William Robison locator; May 22, 1807 recd. this warrant (signed) H Robison.
        no 91, skip in numbers

308 (92). Sept. 10, 1803 Henry G Kearny, assignee of William Haywood assignee of Dixon Marshall assignee of Samuel Murray; warrant 3361; 274 ac on waters of S Harpeth [R], about 2 or 2.5 miles above Alexander's, includes Maple Spring, begins at post oak & chesnut marked as corner, runs S, & W for complement; Robert Davis locator.

309 (93). Sept. 14, 1803 James Robertson; warrant 64; 100 ac on Turnbulls Cr,

on waters of East Fork, includes a spring emptying into a small creek "the first" above Josiah Shipp's, about a mile up the creek from the mouth; Jas Robertson locator.

310 (94). Sept. 15, 1803 Josiah Shipp, assignee of James Robertson; warrant 65; 40 ac in Davidson Co on waters of Turnbulls Cr, on first little creek emptying into main E fork of Turnbulls Cr below here said Shipp lives, on W side of said East fork; Josiah Shipp locator.

311 (95). Sept. 17, 1803 James Hewkins; warrant 507; 640 ac on waters of E fork of Stones [R], on Cripple Cr waters, begins to include improvements William Carter [or Carler] & Joseph "Ship's" improvements (sic), runs for complement; William Mitchell locator; Sept. 22, 1803 this entry removed by me (signed) Wm Mitchell.

312 (96). Sept. 17, 1803 Thomas E Sumner, assignee of William Farn assignee of heirs of Philip Askew; [military] warrant 5263; 640 ac in Middle District on head waters of Stones R "the West fork", begins on "the" Indian line, runs to include sycamore tree marked "HADLY" and another tree marked "W C" standing at head of a large spring and an Indian camp about 50 yards southerly from the spring; Wm Christmas locator; removed Feb. 24, 1803 (signed) Wm Christmas; Apr. 22, 1807 recd. warrant 5263 (signed) Wm Christmas.

313 (97). Sept. 17, 1803 William Harrison, assignee originally of Isaac Waters; [military] warrant 4184; 640 ac, joins Thomas E Sumner's entry on warrant 5263 on East and South "if necessary", & runs according to law for complement; Wm Christmas locator; Apr. 22, 1807 received this warrant (signed) Wm Christmas.

314 (98). Sept. 22, 1803 Charles Gordon; (warrant blank); 400 ac, begins in Indian boundary line 160 poles SW of where said line croses W fork of Stones R, runs N, E, S to said Indian line, & along that to beginning, "first half years pay" [may refer to Evans' Battalion]; William Mitchell locator; Apr. 22, 1807 recd. this warrant (signed) Wm Christmas.

315 (99). Sept. 22, 1803 Charles Gordon; (warrant blank); 400 ac, joins his other 400 ac entry being for his first half years pay on his N boundary, & "if necessary" on his W boundary, second half years pay [may refer to Evans' Battalion]; William Mitchell locator; Apr. 22, 1807 recd. this warrant (signed) Wm Christmas.

316 (100). Sept. 22, 1803 heirs of Wm Sherrod; [military] warrant 3380; 640 ac on waters of E fork of W fork of Stones R, on each side of a creek passing across "the" Indian line, between 8 and 9 mile trees, includes red oak tree 66 poles North of said creek, about 3 miles E of Robert Erwin's SE corner "which tree" is marked "WB"; Wm Christmas locator; Oct. 31, 1803 removed by me (signed) Wm Christmas.

317 (101). Sept. 22, 1803 James Hewkins; warrant 507; 640 ac on W boundary of John Gray & Thomas Blount's 5,000 ac tract on W fork of Stones R, begins between 2 springs near the line, nearly W of Wm Gill's SW corner, runs W, & N for complement; Wm Christmas locator; Apr. 22, 1807 recd. this warrant (signed) Wm Christmas.

318 (102). Sept. 22, 1803 William Vance; warrant 403; 428 ac in Davidson Co on waters of Cripple Cr, a branch of E fork of E fork of Stones R, begins 40 poles E of "whare one" Carter Shipp lives, runs N, S, & W for complement; William Mitchell locator; Jan. 1, 1807 recd. William Vance's warrant 403 for 428 ac (signed) Tho "Mitchel".

319 (103). Sept. 22, 1803 Jonathan Magness, assignee of Thomas Dillon assignee of heirs of John Rainer; [military] warrant 2874; 640 ac in Davidson Co on a branch "supposed" to be waters of Spring Cr, includes part of Recees [or Rices] new Road to Cummins' Mill, runs as law directs for complement; Jonathan Magness locator; Jun. 12, 1806 today I removed this entry & recd. my warrant (signed) Jonathan Magness' mark "X" (witness) Wm Tait.

320 (104). Sept. 23, 1803 Henry Lytle assignee of Howel Tatum; warrant 308; 100 ac on head waters of Dog Cr, begins about 20 yards below the spring, runs as law directs for complement, includes the spring & some marked trees near said spring; Henry Lytle; May 27, 1807 received this warrant (signed) Jno Langham.

321 (105). Sept. 23, 1803 Henry Lytle, assignee of Howel Tatum; warrant 264; 100 ac on head of Sams Cr, begins at "the" spring branch, runs E, S, includes the

spring and vacant land; Henry "Lile" locator; Jan. 20, 1806 today I removed this entry & received my warrant (signed) Henry Lile's mark "X |".

322 (106). Sept. 26, 1803 Wm Davidson, assignee of John Bradly assignee of John Fairman assignee of Wm Gamewell; [military] warrant 3754; 640 ac, West of land now belonging to "one" Rogers on E fork of Stones R, begins 20 poles S of a small spring on E side of a knob, runs as law directs "for &c"; Eph. C Davidson locator.

323 (107). Sept. 27, 1803 Joseph Caldwell, assignee of Howell Tatum; warrant 263; 50.5 ac in Davidson Co on Bluff Cr, about 2.5 miles above mouth of Harpeth [R}, begins on John Bechton's S boundary line, runs up the creek, includes William Boyd's plantation & cobins where he lives, & as law directs for complement; Joseph Caldwell locator; May 25, 1807 received this warrant (signed) Joseph "Calwell".

324 (108). Sept. 30, 1803 Thomas Shute, assignee of James Borland assignee of John & Henry Dunham assignee of Saml Barton assignee of John Dunham heir of Wm Dunham; (warrant blank); 400 ac in Davidson Co on waters of Stewarts Cr, begins on William Green's W boundary line, runs as law directs for complement, includes the best vacant land; Thomas Shute, locator; Apr. 10, 1807 received this warrant No (blank) for 400 ac (signed) Thomas Shute.

325 (109). Oct. 1, 1803 James Hawkins & Obediah M Binge, assignee of Jno W S Mars; (warrant blank); 167.25 ac on waters of "Criple" Cr waters of E fork of Stones R, begins at black oak & dogwood marked with 8 chops each on E side of Taylor's Trace, runs W, & as law directs for complement; (no locator; May 19, 1807 received this warrant (signed) O M Binge.

326 (110). Oct. 11, 1803 Charles Boiles, assignee of William Dickson; warrant 460; 25 ac in Davidson Co on N side of Cumberland R, on waters of Whites Cr, begins on James Marshall's N boundary line 15 poles S of where it crosses the creek, runs N, E for complement, includes the vacant land between D Marshall & others; Charles Boiles locator.
    no 111, skip in numbers

327 (112). Oct. 11, 1803 heirs of Joseph Shearing; warrant 63; 640 ac on waters of E fork of W fork of Stones R, includes a red oak tree marked "WM", runs agreeable to law to include the vacant land; Henry Dyer locator; Apr. 22, 1807 received this warrant (signed) Wm Christmas.

328 (113). Oct. 12, 1803 Joseph Bayer, assignee of William Greenwood assignee of Isaac Curry assignee of Benjamin White assignee of James Davis; (warrant blank); 104 ac in Davidson Co on N side of Stones R, on waters of Suggs Cr, begins on Robert Hays' S boundary line, begins at an ash & dogwood, runs W, S,

includes a small improvement made by Thomas Smothers, & as law directs for complement; Joseph Bayer locator.

329 (114). Oct. 13, 1803 Thomas Shute & "Beal" Bossley, joint assignees of John Maclin assignee of John Herring heir of Jobz Herring; [military] warrant 5059; 640 ac in Davidson Co on Stewarts Cr, on South and East of William Buchanon, runs as law directs, & includes the best vacant land; Thomas Shute locator; Apr. 10, 1807 received above warrant 5039 for 640 ac (not signed) (witness) John C McLemore.

[following 5 items are on 2 sheets, maybe part of book for Second District]
330 (no number). (page torn) made due to part of [John Armstrong] warrant 1119 for 5,000 ac as assignee of William Anderson; surveyed; Lambert Reed; part of warrant 1119 for 5,000 ac; occupant right of 137 ac in Second District, on Reeds Cr, a branch of Elk R, in second fractional secton in fractional range [no number], begins at John Rutledge's beginning corner black oak near foot of Cumberland Mountain "a little" West of Taylor's Trace, runs S45W 230 poles with said Rutledge's line to William Rowark's corner dogwood on bank of said creek, up [East branch of the creek--lined out] meanders of "the same" a conditional line with said W Rowark to large ash on E bank of the creek, E 94 poles to black oak standing at foot of said mountain, with meanders of same binding thereon to beginning; above entry made Aug. 26, 1807 due to part of warrant 1119 for 5,000 ac; Anderson & Strother locators.

331 (no number). "surveyed 787 E P"; this entry made due to warrant 1119 for 200 ac; John Dean 200 ac in White Co on waters of Elk R, in Second District, in section 4 range 9 [written over 3], begins at red oak, runs W & S in a square [no more, bottom sheet].

332 (83). "exd" (no name) as assignee of Joseph Martin, warrant (no number) for 5,000 ac surveyed; Aug. 15, 1807 (page torn) in White Co, Saml Big (page torn) 2 ac due to warrant page torn) in section 1, range (page torn), waters of Boiling Fork of Elk R, includes his improvement as law directs; Samauel Bign(page torn) locator.

333 (84). "exd" surveyed; Aug. 15, 1807 John Clark assignee of John Cockrell; due to part of warrant 56 for 640 ac; 150 ac "in the" 32 poles East of Daniel Barcraft's NE corner, runs S 130 poles, E 160 poles, N 100 poles, W 160 poles, S 80 poles to beginning; (no locator).

334 (85). "exd" this entry made due to part of warrant (page torn) 5,000 ac as assignee of Wm R Anderson, surveyed; Aug. 26, 1807 John King, assignee of Henry Box; 200 ac, as his occupant claim, on waters of Elk R, includes place where he lives, begins on N boundary line of Joseph Box's occupant claim, 40

poles from his NW corner, runs E 180 poles with his line passing his NE corner [at] 20 poles, S 130 poles, W 180 poles, S to beginning; above entry made due to part of warrant 1119 for 5,000 ac; John Strother locator.

series 6 book 8 valid warrants from William Maclin [no page numbers]
[and series 10 book 32: Record of warrants issued by William Maclin, Secretary of State, judged valid in whole or part by Board of Commissioners for East Tennessee]

335. warrant 339 to David Hailey [or Haley] 100 ac; issued due to grant 611 Jul. 12, 1794 to Landon Carter for 500 ac for £0.50 per 100 ac [shuck 771 in Hawkins Co in NC grants}; warrant issued Jun. 6, 1803 by Wm Maclin; Jun. 30, 1807 duplicate, endorsed Jun. 29, 1809, valid for 89 ac, rejected for balance (signed) Archibald Roane, president of East Tennessee Board of Commissioners, (witness) Luke Lea clerk.

336. warrant 338 to David Hailey 100 ac; issued due to grant 611 Jul. 12, 1794 to Landon Carter for 500 ac for £0.50 per 100 ac [shuck 771 in Hawkins Co in NC grants]; warrant issued Jun. 6, 1803 by Wm Maclin; Jun. 30, 1807 duplicate endorsed Jun. 29, 1809, valid for 89 ac & rejected for balance (signed) Archibald Roane, president of East Tennessee Board of Commissioners, (witness) Luke Lea clerk.

337. warrant 23 to Joseph Duncan 100 ac; issued due to grant 920 Nov. 17, 1790 to Joseph Duncan for 200 ac for £0.50 per 100 ac [shuck 943 in Washington Co in NC grants]; warrant issued Jul. 26, 1802 (Knoxville) by Wm Maclin; Aug. 13, 1807 duplicate, valid for 94 ac & rejected for balance 6 ac (signed) Archibald Roane, president of East Tennessee Board of Commissioners (witness) Pat Campbell clerk, warrant transferred by Joseph Duncan to Samuel Johnston.

338. warrant 5 to Francis Mayberry 100 ac; issued due to grant 335 Jun. 27, 1793 for 300 ac to James [Francis--lined out] Mayberry [shuck 457 in Hawkins Co in NC grants]; warrant issued Aug. 8, 1802 by Wm Maclin; warrant assigned by Francis Mayberry to John Evans (signed) Archibald Roane, president of East Tennessee Board of Commissioners, (witness) Pat Campbell clerk.

339. warrant 6 to Francis Mayberry 74 ac; issued due to grant 335 Jun. 27, 1793 for 300 ac to James Mayberry [shuck 457 in Hawkins Co in NC grants]; warrant issued Apr. 8, 1802 (Knoxville) by Wm Maclin; Archibald Roane, president of East Tennessee Board of Commissioners, (witness) Pat Campbell clerk.

340. warrant 7 to Francis Mayberry 26 ac; issued due to grant 335 issued Jun. 27, 1793 for 300 ac to James Mayberry [shuck 457 in Hawkins Co in NC grants]; warrant issued Apr. 8, 1802 (Knoxville) by Wm Maclin; Archibald Roane, president of East Tennessee Board of Commissioners, (witness) Pat Campbell clerk.

341. warrant 354 to Francis Mayberry 150 ac; issued due to grant 133 issued Jun. 24, 1793 to Francis Mayberry for 550 ac for £0.50 per 100 ac [shuck 178 in Eastern Dist in NC grants]; warrant issued Jul. 12, 1803 by Wm Maclin; Archibald

Roane, president of East Tennessee Board of Commissioners, (witness) Pat Campbell clerk; warrant sold by Francis Mayberry to Simeon Huddleston who sold to John Fitzgerral [who sold] to Francis Mayberry.

342. warrant 356 to Francis Mayberry 100 ac; issued due to grant 133 issued Jun. 24, 1793 to Francis Mayberry for 550 ac for £0.50 per 100 ac [shuck 178 in Eastern Dist in NC grants]; warrant issued Jul. 12, 1803 by Wm Maclin; valid for 12 ac, balance rejected (signed) Archibald Roane, president of East Tennessee Board of Commissioners.

343. warrant 355 to Francis Mayberry 100 ac; issued due to grant 133 issued Jun. 24, 1793 to Francis Mayberry for 550 ac for £0.50 per 100 ac [shuck 178 in Eastern Dist in NC grants]; warrant issued Jul. 12 [24--lined out], 1803 by Wm Maclin; duplicate (signed) Archibald Roane, president of East Tennessee Board of Commissioners, (witness) Pat Campbell clerk.

344. warrant 44 to Elijah Chisum [or Chissum] for 50 ac; issued due to grant 733 to Elijah Chisum issued Jul. 20, 1797 for 140 ac for £0.50 per 100 ac [shuck 963 in Hawkins Co in NC grants]; warrant issued Oct. 22, 1802 by Wm Maclin; duplicate, warrant transferred by Elijah Chisum to "Bablist" Church at Cave Spring Meeting House on Roaring River, and transferred by clerk of said Bablist Church Jno Biany to Elijah Chissum; Aug. 24, 1807 valid for full quantity called for in warrant (signed) Archibald Roane, president of East Tennessee Board of Commissioners, (witness) Pat Campbell clerk.

345. warrant 52 to Elijah Chisum [or Chissum] for 100 ac; issued due to grant 303 to Nimrod Dodson issued Mar. 13, 1801 for 1,000 ac for £10 per 100 ac [shuck 4 in Grainger Co in NC grants]; warrant issued Oct. 22, 1802 by Wm Maclin; duplicate, warrant transferred by Elijah Chissum to Sampson Williams; Aug. 24, 1807 judged valid for full quantity called for (signed) Archibald Roane, president of East Tennessee Board of Commissioners, (witness) Pat Campbell clerk.

346. warrant 53 to Elijah Chisum [or Chissum] for 100 ac; issued due to grant 303 to Nimrod Dodson issued Mar. 13, 1801 for 1,000 ac for £10 per 100 ac [shuck 4 in Grainger Co in NC grants]; warrant issued Oct. 22, 1802 by Wm Maclin; warrant assigned by Elijah Chisum to Jesse Starkey; Aug. 24, 1807 valid for 44 ac & rejected for balance (signed) Archibald Roane, president of East Tennessee Board of Commissioners, (witness) Pat Campbell clerk.

347. warrant 50 to Elijah Chisum [or Chissum] for 100 ac; issued due to grant 303 to Nimrod Dodson issued Mar. 13, 1801 for 1,000 ac for £10 per 100 ac [shuck 4 in Grainger Co in NC grants]; warrant issued Oct. 22, 1802 (Knoxville) by Wm Maclin; duplicate, Aug. 24, 1807 warrant assigned by Elijah Chissum to Sampson Williams, judged valid for full quantity called for (signed) Archibald Roane, president of East Tennessee Board of Commissioners, (witness) Pat Campbell

clerk.

348. warrant 51 to Elijah Chisum [or Chissum] for 100 ac; issued due to grant 303 to Nimrod Dodson issued Mar. 13, 1801 for 1,000 ac for £10 per 100 ac [shuck 4 in Grainger Co in NC grants]; warrant issued Oct. 22, 1802 (Knoxville) by Wm Maclin; duplicate, warrant assigned by Elijah Chissum to Stephen Mayfield; Aug. 24, 1807 judged valid for full quantity called for (signed) Archibald Roane, president of East Tennessee Board of Commissioners, (witness) Pat Campbell clerk.

349. warrant 43 to Elijah Chisum [or Chissum] for 50 ac; issued due to grant 733 to Elijah Chisum issued Jul. 20, 1797 for 640 ac for £0.50 per 100 ac [shuck 963 in Hawkins Co in NC grants]; warrant issued Oct. 22, 1802 (Knoxville) by Wm Maclin; duplicate, warrant assigned by Elijah Chisum to Robert Glenn; aug. 24, 1807 judged valid for full quantity in warrant (signed) Archibald Roane, president of East Tennessee Board of Commissioners, (witness) Pat Campbell clerk.

350. warrant 45 to Elijah Chisum [or Chissum] for 50 ac; issued due to grant 733 to Elijah Chisum issued Jul. 20, 1797 for 640 ac for £0.50 per 100 ac [shuck 963 in Hawkins Co in NC grants]; warrant issued Oct. 22, 1802 (Knoxville) by Wm Maclin; duplicate, warrant assigned by Elijah Chisum to William Richardson who sold to Elijah Chisum who sold to Joseph Clark; Aug. 24, 1807 judged valid for 29 ac & rejected for balance (signed) Archibald Roane, president of East Tennessee Board of Commissioners, (witness) Pat Campbell clerk.

[in series 10 book 32:] Jan. 26, 1808 I certify foregoing contains faithful records of warrants issued by William Maclin, Secretary of State, judged valid in whole or part by East Tennessee Board of Commissioners (signed) Archibald Roan, East Tennessee commissioner, A M Lusk, clerk.

350A. [in series 10 book 32 on film] warrant 4 [same as 353 below]

351. warrant 334 to John Adair for 200 ac; issued due to grant 399 to John Adair issued Jul. 29, 1793 for 300 ac for £0.50 per 100 ac [shuck 526 in Hawkins Co in NC grants]; warrant issued Jun. 3, 1803 by Wm Maclin; Apr. 12, 1808 judged valid for full quantity (signed) Archibald Roane, president of East Tennessee Board of Commissioners, (witness) A M Lusk clerk.

351A. [only in series 10 book 22 on film] warrant 333 [same as 354 below]
352. warrant 4 to Francis "Maybery" for 100 ac; issued due to grant 334 to James Mayberry issued Jun. 27, 1793 for 300 ac [maybe shuck 456 in Hawkins Co in NC grants]; warrant issued Apr. 8, 1802 (Knoxville) by Wm Maclin; warrant assigned Jul. 7, 1802 by (omitted) to William Evans for $70 an transferred Mar. 14, 1803 by William Evans to John McDonal [or McDonald] and transferred Mar. 24, 1803 by John McDonald to Benjamin Poor (James Henderson's mark "X" witness) and assigned Oc. 13, 1807 by Benjamin Poor to J Oseph Evans; Jan. 28,

1808 judged valid for 80 ac & invalid for residue being 16 ac (sic) (signed) Archibald Roane, president of East Tennessee Board of Commissioners, (witness) A M Lusk clerk.

353. [lined out, duplicate of 351 above] warrant 334 to John Adair for 100 ac; issued due to grant 399 to John Adair issued Jul. 29, 1793 for 300 ac for £0.50 per 100 ac [shuck 526 in Hawkins Co in NC grants]; warrant issued Jun. 3, 1803 by William Maclin; Apr. 12, 1808 judged valid for full quantity (signed) Archibald Roane, president of East Tennessee Board of Commissioners, (witness) A M Lusk clerk.

354. warrant 333 to John Adair for 100 ac; due to grant 399 to John Adair issued Jul. 29, 1793 for 300 ac for £0.50 per 100 ac [shuck 526 in Hawkins Co in NC grants]; warrant issued Jun. 3, 1803 by Wm Maclin; warrant assigned Oct. 28, 1803 by John Adair to Hezekiah Love; Jul. 14, 1808 judged valid for 81 ac, residue 19 ac rejected (signed) Archibald Roane, president of East Tennessee Board of Commissioners, (witness) A M Lusk clerk.

355. warrant 465 to Isaac Barton for 23.25 ac; due to grant 137 to James Roddy issued Nov. 1, 1786 for 67 ac [shuck 121 in Greene Co in NC grants]; warrant issued Sept. 30, 1803 by Wm Maclin; Oct. 7, 1808 judged valid (signed) Archibald Roane, president of East Tennessee Board of Commissioners, (witness) A M Lusk clerk.

356. warrant 21 to Robert Blackley for 27 ac; due to grant 431 to Robert Blackley issued Oct. 13, 1783 for 100 ac for £0.50 per 100 ac [shuck 439 in Washington Co in NC grants]; warrant issued Jul. 16, 1802 by Wm Maclin; warrant assigned Aug. 2, 1802 (Washington Co, TN) by Robert Blackley to Samuel Adams (Joseph Braun [or Brown] witness); [no more information].

357. warrant 20 to Robert "Blackly" for 100 ac; due to grant 470 issued Oct. 13, 1783 for 100 ac for £0.50 per 100 ac [shuck 478 in Washington Co in NC grants]; warrant issued Jul. 16, 1802 by Wm Maclin; warrant assigned Aug. 12, 1802 by Robert Blackley to William Mitchell (Joseph Brown witness); [no more information].

358. warrant 22 to Robert "Blackly" for 34 ac; due to grant 904 to Robert Blackley issued Nov. 17, 1790 for 200 ac for £0.50 per 100 ac [shuck 927 in Washington Co in NC grants]; warrant issued Jul. 6, 1802 by Wm Maclin; warrant assigned Aug. 26, 1802 by Robert Blackley to David Stuart (Joseph Braun witness); [no more information].

359. warrant 523 to James Roddy for 29.5 ac; due to grant 569 to Abraham Pevehouse [or Pivihause] issued Jul. 12, 1794 for 350 ac for £0.50 per 100 ac [shuck 664 in Hawkins Co in NC grants]; warrant issued Oct. 27, 1803 by Wm

Maclin; [no more information].

360. warrant 81 to Henry Reynalds for 103 ac; due to grant 413 to Henry Reynalds issued Sept. 20, 1787 for 300 ac for £10 per 100 ac [shuck 411 in Greene Co in NC grants]; warrant issued Dec. 6, 1802 by Wm Maclin; [no more information].

361. warrant 83 to Henry Reynalds 33 ac; due to grant 413 to Henry Reynalds issued Sept. 20, 1787 for 300 ac for £10 per 100 ac [shuck 411 in Greene Co in NC grants]; warrant issued Dec. 6, 1802 by Wm Maclin; [no more information].

362. warrant 82 to Henry Reynalds for 82 ac; due to grant 413 to Henry Reynalds issued Sept. 20, 1787 for 300 ac for £10 per 100 ac [shuck 411 in Greene Co in NC grants]; warrant issued Sept. 6, 1802 (Knoxville) by Wm Maclin; [no more information].

363. warrant 448 to Robert Wilson for 50 ac; due to grant 253 to Robert Wilson issued Oct. 24, 1782 for 400 ac for £0.50 per 100 ac [shuck 85 in Washington Co in NC grants]; warrant issued Sept. 14, 1803 by Wm Maclin; warrant assigned Nov. 8, 1805 by John Adams, attorney for executor of Robert Wilson, to Walker Barin (Nathan Shiply witness); Jul. 2, 1809 judged valid for 42 ac 20 poles, residue rejected (signed) Archibald Roane, president of East Tennessee Board of Commissioners, (witness) A M Lusk clerk.

364. warrant 335 to David Haily for 16 ac; due to grant 612 to Landon Carter issued Jul. 12, 1794 for 500 ac for £0.50 per 100 ac [shuck 772 in Hawkins Co in NC grants]; warrant issued Jun
. 6, 1803 by Wm Maclin; Jun. 2, 1809 judged valid for full quantity (signed) Archibald Roane, president of East Tennessee Board of Commissioners, (witness) Andw M Lusk clerk.

365. warrant 336 to David Haily for 100 ac; due to grant 612 to Landon Carter issued Jul. 12, 1794 for 500 ac for £0.50 per 100 ac [shuck 772 in Hawkins Co in NC grants]; warrant issued Jun. 6, 1803 by Wm Maclin; Jun. 2, 1809 judged valid for 55 ac, residue of 45 ac rejected (signed) Archibald Roane, president of East Tennessee Board of Commissioners, (witness) Andw M Lusk clerk.

366. warrant 447 to Robert Wilson for 125 ac; due to grant 253 to Robert Wilson issued Oct. 24, 1782 for $400 for £0.50 per 100 ac [shuck 85 in Washington Co in NC grants]; warrant issued Sept. 14, 1803 by Wm Maclin; Oct 14, 1803 warrant sold by John Adams, attorney for John Crawford executor of Robert Wilson deceased, to David Kennedy (Joseph Britton witness); Jun. 2, 1809 judged valid for full quantity (signed) Archibald Roane, president of East Tennessee Board of Commissioners, (witness) Andw M Lusk clerk.

367. Aug. 2, 1809 preceeding examined & "conected"

Nov. 18, 1809 I certify foregoing is true copy of recorded valid warrants issued by William Maclin (signed) Archibald Roane, president of East Tennessee Board of Commissioners, (witness) Andw M Lusk clerk.

368. warrant 29 to Nathan Shiply for 53 ac; due to grant 1043 to John Beam issued Nov. 27, 1792 for 153 ac for £0.50 per 10 ac [may be shuck 1093 to John "Bean" in Washington Co in NC grants]; warrant issued Aug. 19, 1802 by Wm Maclin; Jul. 3, 1810 duplicate of warrant to issue to Nathan Shiply due to act of Assembly for relief of certain persons mentioned passed Nov. 22, 1809 (signed) Archibald Roane, president of East Tennessee Board of Commissioners, (witness) Andw M Lusk clerk.

369. warrant 516 to Robert S [or T] Brashears for 6 ac; due to grant 409 to Robert S "Brashier" issued Aug. 9, 1787 for 300 ac for £0.50 per 100 ac [shuck 270 in Sullivan Co in NC grants]; warrant issued Oct. 25, 1803 by Wm Maclin; Jul. 4, 1810 judged valid (signed) Archibald Roane, president of East Tennessee Board of Commissioners, (witness) Andrew M Lusk clerk; warrant assigned Aug. 30, 1805 by Robert S Brashears to William N Gale (John Anderson witness).

370. warrant 28 to Nathan Shiply for 100 ac; due to grant 1043 to John Beam issued Nov. 2, 1792 for 153 ac for £0.50 per 100 ac [may be shuck 1093 to John Bean in Washington Co in NC grants]; warrant issued Aug. 19, 1802 by Wm Maclin; Jul. 3, 1810 duplicate warrant to issue to Nathan Shiply due to third section of act of Assembly for relief of certain persons named passed Nov. 22, 1809 (signed) Archibald Roane, president of East Tennessee Board of Commissioners, (witness) Andrew M Lusk clerk; warrant assigned Aug. 23, 1802 by
Nathan Shiply to "Ezekiel" Lyon (John Chapman witness
).

371. warrant
165 to Thomas Stanfield for 86 ac; due to grant 503 to Thomas Stanfield issued Sept. 20, 1787 for 300 ac for £10 per 100 ac [shuck 501 in Greene Co in NC grants]; warrant issued Apr. 8, 1803 by Wm Maclin; Jul. 4, 1810 judged valid for full quantity (signed) Archibald Roane, president of East Tennessee Board of Commissioners, (witness) Andrew M Lusk clerk; warrant sold Apr. 26, 1803 by Thomas Stanfield to Henry Farnsworth sr (Jas Temple witness).

372. warrant 166 to Thomas Stanfield for 147 ac; due to grant 503 to Thomas Stanfield
issued Sept. 20, 1787 for 300 ac for £10 per 100 ac [shuck 501 in Greene Co in NC grants]; warrant
issued Apr. 8,

1803 by Wm Maclin; Jul. 4, 1810 judged valid for 139 ac, residue 8 ac rejected (signed) Archibald Roane, president of East Tennessee Board of Commissioners, (witness) Andrew M Lusk clerk; warrant transferred Apr. 26, 1803 by Thomas Stanfield to Henry Farnsworth sr (Jas Temple witenss).

373. warrant 164 to Thomas Stanfield for 67 ac; due to grant 503 to Thomas Stanfield issued Sept. 20, 1787 for 300 ac for £10 per 100 ac [shuck 501 in Greene Co in NC grants]; warrant issued Apr. 8, 1803 by Wm Maclin; Jul. 4, 1810 judged valid for whole quantity called for (signed) Archibald Roane, president of East Tennessee Board of Commissioners, (witness) Andrew M Lusk clerk; warrant transferred Apr. 26, 1803 by Thomas Stanfield to James Peirce (Jas Temple witness) and transferred Feb. 13, 1810 by James "Pearce" to Henry Farnsworth sr (James Temple witness).

374. Nov. 23, 1810 I certify from No. 29 to No. 164 are coies of warrants issued by Secretary of State judged valid between Nov. 18, 1809 and Nov. 23, 1810 (signed) Archibald Roane, president of East Tennessee Board of Commissioners, (witness) Andrew M Lusk clerk.

375. warrant 183 to Asahel Rawlings for 100 ac; due to grant 441 to Asahel Rawlings issued Oct. 13, 1783 for 268 ac for £0.50 per 100 ac [shuck 449 in Washington Co in NC grants]; warrant issued May 2, 1803 by Wm Maclin; (Knoxville) Nov. 24, 1814 duplicate (signed) Archibald Roane, president of East Tennessee Board of Commissioners, (witness) William C Mynatt clerk; warrant assigned May 2, 1803 by Asahel Rawlings to Robert Hinson (Wm Maclin witness).

376. warrant 182 to Asahel Rawlings for 17 ac; due to grant 441 to Asahel Rawlings issued Oct. 13, 1783 for 268 ac for £0.50 per 100 ac [shuck 449 in Washington Co in NC grants]; warrant issued May 2, 1803 by Wm Maclin; (Knoxville) Dec. 20, 1814 duplicate (signed) Nathan Shipley, commissioner for East Tennessee, (witness) William C Mynatt clerk; May 2, 1803 warrant assigned by Asahel Rawlings to John Hagey (Wm Maclin witness) and assigned May 12, 1803 by John Hagey's mark "X" to George Ault (R Houston witness).

377. Sept. 8, 1815 this is to certify foregoing warrants No. 183 and 182 are correctly recorded (signed) Nathan Shipley, commissioner for East Tennessee, (witness) William C Mynatt clerk; [rest of page blank].

Land Entries of Jackson County & Davidson County, TN (1802-1803)

Road, wagon 136, 146, 185
Road, Walton's 152
Run, Cub 152
Run, Sugar 29
Section 1, range (blank) 332
Section 4, range 9 331
Sheriff, the 24
Shuck, DC2468A 278
Shuck, ED178 341-343
Shuck, ED508 74, 151
Shuck, GR4 345-348
Shuck, GE121 355
Shuck, GE411 360-362
Shuck, HW456 352
Shuck, HW457 338
Shuck, HW501 371-373
Shuck, HW526 351, 353, 354
Shuck, HW664 359
Shuck, HW771 335, 336
Shuck, HW772 364, 365
Shuck, HW963 344, 349, 350
Shuck, MD219 119
Shuck, SN470 153
Shuck, SU270 369
Shuck, WA85 363, 366
Shuck, WA439 356
Shuck, WA449 375, 376
Shuck, WA478 357
Shuck, WA927 358
Shuck, WA943 337
Shuck, WA1093 368, 370
Spring, alam 197
Spring, cane 184
Spring, E Coock's 207
Spring, Glavens 182
Spring, Hart's 297
Spring, Isom's 186
Spring, J Anderson's 210
Spring, J Foxe's 210
Spring, Maple 308
Spring, Mayfield's 204
Spring, Otter 289
Spring, Parris 146
Spring, Rocky 34
Spring, Sink hole 18, 268, 284, 297
Spring, sinking 125, 179
Spring, Sycamore 198
Spring, the 2, 23, 44, 47, 74, 122,
    142, 157, 159, 165, 173, 185, 189,
    191, 257, 270, 279, 294, 309, 312,

    317, 320-322
Spring, Trouble 126
Spring, W Bradley's 208
Survey, Mansker's Lick 261, 262
Tennessee, Davidson Co 240-329
Tennessee, Hawkins Co 338
Tennessee, Jackson Co 1-239
Tennessee, Knoxville 337, 339,
    340, 347-350, 362, 375, 376
Tennessee, Middle Dist 312
Tennessee, Nashville 283
Tennessee, Second Dist 330-334
Tennessee, White Co 331, 332
Tennessee, Williamson 240
Trace, Taylor's 325, 330
Trunk, maker 206
Valley, the 39, 53
Wararnt, 63 327
Warrant, (no number) 1, 2, 6-11,
    14-23, 28, 93, 109, 183, 254, 259,
    279, 314, 315, 324, 325, 328, 332
Warrant, 4 139
Warrant, 6 138, 296
Warrant, 8 248
Warrant, 9 249
Warrant, 10 252
Warrant, 11 250
Warrant, 14 251, 295
Warrant, 23 283
Warrant, 39 208
Warrant, 44 184
Warrant, 56 333
Warrant, 64 309
Warrant, 65 310
Warrant, 69 265
Warrant, 70 266
Warrant, 71 263
Warrant, 72 144, 264
Warrant, 73 268, 298
Warrant, 74 267
Warrant, 84 277
Warrant, 85 276
Warrant, 86 275
Warrant, 87 274
Warrant, 88 293
Warrant, 92 292
Warrant, 93 287
Warrant, 97 278
Warrant, 98 300
Warrant, 99 301

Warrant, MA1101 57
Warrant, MA1233 123
Warrant, MA1321 79
Warrant, MA1432 13
Warrant, MA1440 78
Warrant, MA1457 5
Warrant, MA1476 86
Warrant, MA1509 306
Warrant, MA1520 107
Warrant, MA1923 75
Warrant, MA1932 3, 4
Warrant, MA2100 24
Warrant, MA2287 167
Warrant, MA2288 30
Warrant, MA2320 133
Warrant, MA2439 261
Warrant, MA2464 125
Warrant, MA2676 153
Warrant, MA2808 193
Warrant, MA2869 233
Warrant, MA2871 236
Warrant, MA2874 319
Warrant, MA2876 285
Warrant, MA2883 297
Warrant, MA2885 185
Warrant, MA2937 191
Warrant, MA2995 271
Warrant, MA2997 244
Warrant, MA3017 26
Warrant, MA3021 304
Warrant, MA3274 243
Warrant, MA3285 192, 2387
Warrant, MA3361 308
Warrant, MA3380 316
Warrant, MA3383 66, 84, 108, 209
Warrant, MA3553 60, 88, 89
Warrant, MA3635 43
Warrant, MA3636 227
Warrant, MA3730 216
Warrant, MA3741 97
Warrant, MA3754 322
Warrant, MA3761 55, 102, 106, 116
Warrant, MA3773 247
Warrant, MA3793 240
Warrant, MA3937 171
Warrant, MA3954 169
Warrant, MA3960 45, 169, 187
Warrant, MA3987 269
Warrant, MA3992 256

Warrant, MA3993 255
Warrant, MA4046 76
Warrant, MA4060 75
Warrant, MA4090 262, 288
Warrant, MA4131 211
Warrant, MA4132 24, 151
Warrant, MA4184 313
Warrant, MA4215 46
Warrant, MA4223 75
Warrant, MA4225 221
Warrant, MA4295 258, 280
Warrant, MA4303 246
Warrant, MA4308 253, 302
Warrant, MA4328 44, 168
Warrant, MA4338 186, 213
Warrant, MA4447 64
Warrant, MA4495 215
Warrant, MA4701 131
Warrant, MA4711 178
Warrant, MA4737 245
Warrant, MA4787 241
Warrant, MA4791 242
Warrant, MA5010 257
Warrant, MA5059 329
Warrant, MA5103 114, 114A, 115
Warrant, MA5104 83
Warrant, MA5111 152, 153
Warrant, MA5112 305
Warrant, MA5157 210
Warrant, MA5160 235
Warrant, MA5174 163, 165
Warrant, MA5193 25, 227
Warrant, MA5203 92, 132
Warrant, MA5220 220
Warrant, MA5239 272
Warrant, MA5263 312, 313
Warrant, MA5285 273
Warrant, WC1 112
Warrant, WM4 350A, 352
Warrant, WM5 338
Warrant, WC16 170
Warrant, WC26 113
Warrant, WC38 119
Warrant, WC41 212
Warrant, WC43 260
Warrant, WC49 196
Warrant, WC57 120-122
Warrant, WC65 194
Warrant, WC85 195
Warrant, WM6 339